Information Technology and Law Series

Volume 41

The *Information Technology and Law Series* was an initiative of IT*e*R, the national programme for information Technology and Law, which was a research programme set up by the Dutch government and The Netherlands Organisation for Scientific Research (NWO) in The Hague. Since 1995 IT*e*R has published all of its research results in its own book series. In 2002 IT*e*R launched the present internationally orientated and English language *Information Technology and Law Series.* This well-established series deals with the implications of information technology for legal systems and institutions. Manuscripts and related correspondence can be sent to the Series' Editorial Office, which will also gladly provide more information concerning editorial standards and procedures.

Laurensia Andrini

Protecting Artificial Intelligence-generated Works in Indonesia

Insights from the European Union Approach

ASSER PRESS

Springer

Laurensia Andrini
Faculty of Law, Business Law Department
Universitas Gadjah Mada
Yogyakarta, Indonesia

ISSN 1570-2782 ISSN 2215-1966 (electronic)
Information Technology and Law Series
ISBN 978-94-6265-702-1 ISBN 978-94-6265-703-8 (eBook)
https://doi.org/10.1007/978-94-6265-703-8

This work was supported by the Australia Awards Scholarship/Faculty of Law, Universitas Gadjah Mada.

Published by T.M.C. ASSER PRESS, The Hague, The Netherlands www.asserpress.nl
Produced and distributed for T.M.C. ASSER PRESS by Springer-Verlag Berlin Heidelberg

This T.M.C. ASSER PRESS imprint is published by the registered company Springer-Verlag GmbH, DE, part of Springer Nature.
The registered company address is: Heidelberger Platz 3, 14197 Berlin, Germany

To Ozzi, Oswald and Redwald

Acknowledgements

The author would like to thank Dr. Allison Fish and Professor Brad Sherman from the University of Queensland, Australia, who have provided useful guidance in developing this manuscript. Dr. Fish and Professor Sherman also played pivotal roles in keeping this manuscript consistent and logical.

Contents

Abbreviations and Symbols

AI	Artificial Intelligence
AUD	Australian dollar
BBC	British Broadcasting Company
BPPT	*Badan Pengkajian dan Penerapan Teknologi*
CD	Compact Disc
CEO	Chief Executive Officer
CERN	European Council for Nuclear Research
CMO	Collective Management Organisation
COVID-19	Coronavirus Disease 2019
DSM	Digital Single Market
EU	European Union
EUR	Euro
GANs	Generative Adversarial Networks
GATT	General Agreement on Tariffs and Trade
GDP	Gross Domestic Products
GSP	Generalised System of Preferences
HBO	Home Box Office
IDR	Indonesian Rupiah
IFPV	International Federation of Phonogram and Videogram
IIPA	International Intellectual Property Alliance
IP	Intellectual Property
LLM	Large Language Model
NCMO	National Collective Management Organisation
NRIA	National Research and Innovation Agency
TCE	Traditional Cultural Expressions
TKTCE	Traditional Knowledge and Traditional Cultural Expressions
TRIPs	Trade-Related Aspects of Intellectual Property Rights
TV	Television
UK	United Kingdom
US	United States
USA	United States of America

USD	United States dollar
USTR	United States Trade Representative
VCD	Video Compact Disc
VHS	Video Home System
WIPO	World Intellectual Property Organization
WTO	World Trade Organization

List of Figures

Chapter 1
Comparative Approaches to Copyright Protection for AI-generated Works in the European Union and Indonesia

Contents

Abstract Generative artificial intelligence and its ability to produce works mimicking human creation has challenged copyright law throughout the world, including both Indonesia's and the European Union (EU)'s. These jurisdictions are required to address two primary questions, namely whether artificial intelligence-generated works can be granted copyright protection, and, if so, who should be granted ownership over these works. This chapter explains the similarity between Indonesia's copyright law to a widely recognised copyright concept in the EU, namely its requirement of originality and moral rights concept that is strongly recognised in both the EU Member States and Indonesia, and argues that due to these similarities, Indonesia may have a similar approach in responding to the challenge brought by generative AI. Additionally, it also explains that Indonesia is an interesting site of exploration because, as a middle-income country that regularly participates in and influences the development of global intellectual property law, an account addressing Indonesia's legal requirements, norms, and values will contribute new perspectives to a scholarly debate that is overwhelmingly focused on developed countries.

Keywords Copyright · Generative AI · AI-generated works · Originality · Authorship · Indonesian copyright · EU copyright · Middle-income country · WTO

L. Andrini, *Protecting Artificial Intelligence-generated Works in Indonesia*, Information Technology and Law Series 41, https://doi.org/10.1007/978-94-6265-703-8_1

1.1 Challenges Posed by Artificial Intelligence-generated Works to Copyright Law

Technological innovations have continually challenged how copyright law operates, thus generating numerous debates regarding how this legal domain might shift to accommodate these new advances. In this vein, scholarly accounts document the dramatic contests triggered by introducing numerous forms of recording technology, such as the phonograph, cable broadcasting, and VHS players.[1] These devices upended the norms and assumptions informing significant principles and concepts in copyright law at the time of their introduction. Specifically, these technologies allowed users to access and enjoy repeated playbacks of protected works without obtaining permission from the copyright holder in new ways.[2] In these cases, and numerous others, technological advances have made it difficult for the copyright holder to control the circulation of the protected work, thereby presenting a potential free rider problem.[3] In other situations, new technologies not only increased the ease with which protected materials were circulated and consumed, but also removed the distinction between producers and consumers of content.[4] Prime examples of these types of innovations include the recording tape player and internet-based peer-to-peer communication technologies; both of which allowed users to copy, record, remix, and circulate protected materials.[5] In these cases, new forms of technology changed how creative works were produced, as well as who was involved in their production. Taken as a whole, these technological and social changes have fundamentally challenged the core legal logics and requirements of copyright. As a consequence, the law has shifted, expanded and changed to accommodate the resulting socio-technical transformations.[6]

Similar shifts in copyright law are at play today due to the development and increasing availability of generative artificial intelligence (AI) systems capable of producing objects mimicking human creativity (hereinafter, for purposes of simplicity 'AI-generated works'). Well known examples of generative AI systems capable of producing AI-generated works include *ChatGPT, DALL-E, Midjourney,* and AIVA – all of which can be easily accessed over the internet and can be used

[1] See Lessig 2001, pp. 107–11.

[2] See Hugenholtz 2012, pp. 179–196; Sherman and Wiseman 2012. See also Boyle 2003; Schaumann 1983.

[3] A "free rider" in this case is seen as anyone who obtains (a) benefit(s) from someone else's investment. In the relation between technological advance and copyright, copying digital files and selling them to the public without approval from the original copyright holder can be an example of free riding.

[4] See Swire 2008.

[5] Included in these examples are Apple's advertisement of "Rip, mix, burn" that invites consumers not only to enjoy the music but to take part in ripping, mixing, and burning such a remix into records, see Lessig 2001.

[6] While the development of recording technology and peer-to-peer file sharing challenge the idea of fixation and/or the introduction of a broadcast licensing fee, the presence of AI-generated works created by ML software presents questions on the authorship and creativity requirement of copyright.

by non-specialist audiences. In exploring these shifts, this book specifically focuses on the Indonesian context, with some insights from the EU, and considers how these jurisdictions might reshape domestic copyright policy as well as contribute to the larger global debate on whether AI-generated works belong in the public or private domain.

Generative AI is a sophisticated branch of computational research that is noted for producing systems with the ability to learn patterns from existing datasets and to use these models to produce new outcomes.[7] Recent advances have made it possible for generative AI to produce creative works of an artistic value that were previously considered the unique province of human ingenuity and authorship.[8] In this way, generative AI systems have the capacity to challenge copyright law as did previous technological innovations, which similarly tested what were, at the time of their release and adoption, widely accepted notions relating to the production, circulation, and consumption of creative works. However, generative AI systems differ from previous technological innovations because these technologies introduce wholly new actors into the creative process. These new actors include software developers, software users, and data aggregators and trainers - all of whom have may invest significant resources into the production of the resulting AI-generated works and who also have the potential to leave an imprint upon AI-generated works.[9] As such, questions arise as to whether the interests of these new stakeholders need to be taken into account when determining whether and how copyright protection might apply to AI-generated works.

Whether computer software can or should produce works that attract copyright protection has been anticipated by legal scholars and policy makers since the 1980s. However, the computing technologies involved in producing AI-generated works have fundamentally changed since these debates began. Some of the earlier discussions, which were predicated upon simpler technologies, identified software user as the suitable copyright holder. For example, Pamela Samuelson, an early scholar of law and technology, foresaw the use of computational technologies to produce works capable of mimicking human creativity. In her early work, Samuelson (1985) asserted that a software user is equivalent to an author since both perform the fixation of a work[10] and, as a result, should be the natural holder of copyright interests in the resulting work.[11] However, Samuelson proposed this solution in 1985 when software generally had significantly lower autonomy than contemporary generative AI. In this situation, a software user had significant input into the operation of a computational

[7] Grant and Wischik 2020, p. x.

[8] One of the most well-known examples of the use of AIs to produce AI-generated works is the painting called '*Le Comte de Belamy*' which was sold for almost half a million dollars at an auction in 2018, see Quackenbush 2018.

[9] AI-generated works refer to any digital art produced by using generative AI technology.

[10] A work is considered fixed when it is recorded to or stored in a medium so that it can be perceived, reproduced, and communicated.

[11] Samuelson 1986.

system and was often more readily identifiable.[12] Recently, the amplified capacity and complexity of software systems has increased the number of potential contributors, both human and machine, involved in the creation of works, thus making it difficult to distinguish and assign authorship. Recent scholarly debates suggest that authorship could be assigned to software developers, data aggregators and trainers,[13] or even the generative AI system itself,[14] while also suggesting that AI-generated works should not receive copyright protection and must proceed immediately to the public domain.[15] Given this contention, long-standing assumptions about legal concepts, particularly 'originality', 'creativity', and 'human authorship', may need to be reassessed if the question of copyright and AI-generated works is to be resolved.[16]

Given that there is no clear and widely acceptable solution to the question of copyright in AI-generated works nor a clear lead at the international level, unsurprisingly various jurisdictions have developed different approaches in recent years. Some Commonwealth countries, including the United Kingdom, New Zealand, India, and Hong Kong, assign copyright to the person making the 'arrangements necessary' for the work'.[17] While this phrasing opens the possibility for AI-generated works to attract copyright protection, it falls short of clarifying the parameters of 'arrangements necessary'. Meanwhile, there are also some jurisdictions that have changing ideas on protecting AI-generated works with copyright. In 2021, the United States Copyright Office stipulated that copyright protection should only be given to works

---

[12] Samuelson gives an example of how an architect's role, as a software user, may still be needed in software that generates architectural plans. She asserts that:

> "For example, a programmer may have worked with an experienced architect (or group of architects) to develop a program capable of generating architectural plans. The programmer himself may not be an architect, and may not be able to use his own program to create a comparable architectural design that an experienced architect using the program could develop with its aid." In ibid.

[13] Lim 2018; Yu 2017; Huson 2018.

[14] Yanisky-Ravid and Velez-Hernandez 2018; Abbott 2016.

[15] Scholars who argue that AI-generated works should go directly into the public domain based their argument on achieving a balance between private and public benefits. Mark Perry and Thomas Margoni, for example, argued that the public-private balance has been disturbed by the fact that public interests only play a small part in society. Should copyright be given to AI-generated works, such public interests would be eroded and therefore the equilibrium could not be achieved, in Perry and Margoni 2010, p. 629.

[16] Andrew Ventimiglia proposes an '*a posteriori*' model of authorship that acknowledges authorship as mediumship. This model firstly acknowledges the emergence of the work as a legal-material object; and proceeds with a legal analysis on who the author might be. This proposal was based on the analysis of *Urantia v. Maaherra*, a dispute over *The Urantia Book* that was believed to have been created by multiple authors involving divine spirits as authors and human beings as mediums. Ventimiglia argued that the creation of *The Urantia Book* may share similarities with the creation of AI-generated works in the sense that 1) there are multiple authors involved; and 2) one or more of the authors are non-human entities (Ventimiglia 2020).

[17] White and Matulionyte 2020, p. 207.

directly produced by human authors. Consequently, AI-generated works were automatically placed in the public domain upon creation.[18] However, in March 2023, the United States Copyright Office altered its position by allowing copyright protection for AI-generated works providing that the works contain human authorship.[19] In short, the legal landscape surrounding the question of copyright in AI generated works continues to be heterogenous and shifting as these technological systems become more prevalent. Furthermore, this is true not only for questions of copyright, specifically, but also for the other legal domains that are implicated in the regulation of this new and emerging technology. For example, the United States Senate called a hearing on 16 May 2023 to review legal concerns pertaining to AI systems during which Sam Altman, CEO of *ChatGPT*, asserted the industry and societal need for greater regulatory clarity across numerous domains from intellectual property to individual health and financial privacy to national and global security to misinformation/ disinformation through to other areas.

In the area of copyright and generative AI, heterogenous and shifting domestic policies have emerged which have contributed to the confusion. For example, in 2023 the United States Copyright Office announced a near reversal of its previous position; which derived from a rule the agency had adopted just two years earlier in 2021. This instability shows that instead of looking for long-term legal solutions for the challenge raised by the rapid development of AI, lawmakers have tended to establish temporary and, sometimes, ill-informed resolutions. Unfortunately, these temporary responses function only as legal patches to a rapidly changing socio-technological eco-system that has a high potential to change in the future following technological development.

In many respects, the scenario described above demonstrates the difficulty that the law and law-making institutions have in attempting to keep up with and respond to socio-technical change, broadly, as well as the specific shifts that have been and will be triggered by generative AI. As suggested by David Friedman, new technology often produces novel circumstances that cannot be adequately addressed by existing legal logics and that, in this scenario, legal change is required.[20] This is also true for the operation of modern copyright, a domain of law whose popular rationale is based on the notion that authors need economic incentives to create and, therefore, should receive compensation for their works to encourage the enrichment of the knowledge commons. Such rationale, however, is not only challenged by some research,[21] but also does not directly map onto the processes at play in the generation of AI-generated works, which do not necessarily require an economic incentive to

---

[18] *U.S. Copyright Office, Compendium of the United States Copyright Office Practices* (US Copyright Compendium), sct 313.2.

[19] *Copyright Registration Guidance: Works Containing Material Generated by Artificial Intelligence, Federal Register* (US Copyright Registration Guidance: Works Containing Material Generated by Artificial Intelligence), Vol. 88, No. 51.

[20] Friedman 2001, pp. 71–75.

[21] Roberta Rosenthal Kwall, for example, suggests that there is an intrinsic motivation for an author to create works, such as 'challenge, personal satisfaction, or the creation of works with particular meaning or significance for the author,' (Kwall 2006, p. 1947). Further, Zimmerman asserts that

operate. Further, while copyright generally requires human authorship to subsist in a work, AI-generated works are often created either autonomously by a generative AI system or through collaboration between generative AI systems and human authors. As such, copyright is challenged to establish whether authorship can be adapted to the autonomous nature of generative AI.

Despite the exponential speed with which information technology develops, a stable and consistent rule is desirable to guarantee legal certainty, thus warranting two requirements. First, legal certainty requires the law to be clear, accessible, and reliable.[22] Second, legal certainty guarantees that people's legitimate expectation of the law is met according to consistent policy.[23] As such, rapidly shifting, unclear, and conflicting policies as exemplified by US copyright policies that reference AI-generated works, can potentially create legal uncertainty.[24]

We can learn two things from the United States example of shifting policy. First, legal certainty does not require static and unchanging policy. At the same time, consistent policy is often desirable so that anyone who may feel the impact of the policy knows what to do and expect from the law. The 2023 US Copyright Registration Guidelines have actually been consistent with the 2021 Copyright Compendium by requiring human authorship for copyright protection, and refusing to protect works made solely by generative AI. The second point applies to the importance of basing policy upon sound evidence.[25] The United States 2023 Copyright Registration Guidelines were introduced after accounting for new and emerging uses of generative AI. The Guidelines consider the possibility of human-generative AI collaboration in producing works, and human author's contribution in selecting, arranging or modifying AI-generated works in a way that requires human creativity.[26] As a result, the Guidelines devised the policy not to be as rigid as the 2021 Copyright Compendium, yet still to remain consistent with copyright law. Reviewing the approach in the United States' example reveals that, because developing AI-related technology is often unpredictable, it requires current situations and future predictions to be thoroughly investigated before a successful legal response can be established.

---

authors' production of works is often more of 'a product of love than as a response to the promise of money,' see Zimmerman 2011, p. 34.

[22] Popelier 2017.

[23] Ibid.

[24] In 2021, the United States Copyright Compendium mentioned that copyright will protect only original works of human authorship and reject those produced by a machine or mechanical processes that work autonomously without any human intervention. This policy insinuates that AI-generated works cannot be in any way protected by the US copyright law. However, in 2023, the United States Copyright Registration Guideline stated that works containing material produced by generative AI may still be protected as long as the applicant can establish the presence of human authorship. It implies that, as long as a human intervention selects, modifies or arranges the works, they can be registered for and protected by copyright, see US Copyright Compendium, above n. 18.

[25] Moses 2003.

[26] US Copyright Registration Guidance: Works Containing Material Generated by Artificial Intelligence, above n. 19.

This book is focused on finding the best approach to protect AI-generated works in Indonesia by taking into consideration the approach adopted by the European Union (EU). By examining the EU's legal frameworks and policies, which are among the most advanced in addressing the intricacies of generative AI, this book aims to identify strategies that can be adapted to the Indonesian context. It is looking at EU example to ensure that AI-generated works are protected, fostering a conducive environment for technological advancement in Indonesia.

1.2 The European Union's Approach to AI-generated Works

The EU's legal framework for copyright includes directives applicable to all Member States, including the Information Society Directive 29/2001/EC (InfoSoc); Software Directive 2009/24/EC; Database Directive 96/9/EC and the Term Directive 2006/116 EC. Throughout these directives it can be inferred that copyright in the EU is deemed as a reward for the authors for their labour and investment.[27] Additionally, the standard of copyright protection in the EU is based on its compliance to the Berne Convention, which requires that the work should be original, created by an author, and fixated in a medium.[28] Therefore, AI-generated works could not meet EU's standard of copyright protection for two main reasons. First, these works are produced by a non-human entity. It makes them unable to satisfy the authorship requirement, which necessitates a human author.[29] Second, they do not meet the originality requirement because the creators of AI-generated works do not make free and creative choices. [30] Instead, it only involves an algorithmic process that follows rules and boundaries set by its programmers.

The EU has been proactive in addressing the legal challenges posed by AI-generated works. In 2020, European Parliament published resolution on intellectual property rights for the development of AI. It urges the European Commission to regulate intellectual property rights protection for AI-generated works because it realises that the development AI may raise questions on the ownership of AI-generated works.[31] In terms of copyright, the lack of human authorship in AI-generated works challenges the core principle of copyright, which is designed to protect human authors. This is why the parliament suggests that any proprietary rights over AI-generated works should be attributed to the person who contributes to

---

[27] *Directive 2001/29/EC of the European Parliament and Council on the Harmonisation of Certain Aspects of Copyright and Related Rights in the Information Society.*

[28] Article 2, and Article 3., *The Berne Convention for the Protection of Literary and Artistic Works as amended on 28 September 1979.*

[29] Hugenholtz and Quintais 2021, p. 1194.

[30] *Case C-145/10 Painer [2011] ECLI:EU:C:2011:798*, para 88–90.

[31] *European Parliament, Intellectual property rights for the development of artificial intelligence technologies, 2020/2015(INI), 2020 O.J.* (C 338).

the creation of the work.[32] In this resolution, the parliament also calls for a mandatory labelling system to indicate the degree of human contribution in the AI-generated works.[33]

In April 2021, the EU proposed the draft of Artificial Intelligence Act. This draft regulates the transparency, accountability and human oversight of AI systems.[34] It focuses on classifying AI systems based on the risk they possess. It prohibits 'dangerous' AI systems and gives additional measures to high-risk AI, so that their use does not breach the safety and fundamental rights of EU citizens.[35] EU AI Act primarily focuses on regulating how AI might and might not be used in the EU. It does not specifically address ownership of AI-generated works. With regards to copyright, the Act does, however, requires transparency on the datasets used to train AI models, which may be copyrighted materials.[36]

1.3 Indonesia's Approach to AI-generated Works

To date, Indonesia has not addressed the question of copyright protection for AI-generated works. As an emerging economy in South-East Asia with a rapidly developing information technology sector, Indonesia has national priorities that may be different from those of Member States in the EU; the jurisdictions upon which most research is focused. In focusing on Indonesia, the book highlights different perspectives and generates new insights into how AI-generated works might be regulated under copyright law. In engaging with these questions, the research analyses the interplay between law, technology and society within the Indonesian context. It highlights both the necessity of considering AI-generated works as new objects of protection in Indonesian copyright law and argues that any changes in the law should reflect the expectations and understandings of relevant experts including software developers, data trainers and software users

In finding the most suitable strategies to accommodate AI-generated works into copyright law, I explore several options, as shown in Fig. 1.1.

The first option is to deny any form of proprietary rights over AI-generated works thus leaving them in the public domain. Supporters of this argument believe that AI-generated works are produced automatically without any human intervention or creativity.[37] This, as I will show, is not an accurate reflection of how AI-generated works are created. As is discussed in Chap. 2, their creation needs contributions from

[32] Number 15, C 338, above n. 31.

[33] Number 9, ibid.

[34] *European Parliament, Proposal for a Regulation of the European Parliament and of the Council Laying Down Harmonised Rules on Artificial Intelligence* (Artificial Intelligence Act) *and Amending Certain Union Legislative Acts, COM/2021/206.*

[35] Articles 5 and 6, ibid.

[36] Article 54, ibid.

[37] See Perry and Margoni 2010.

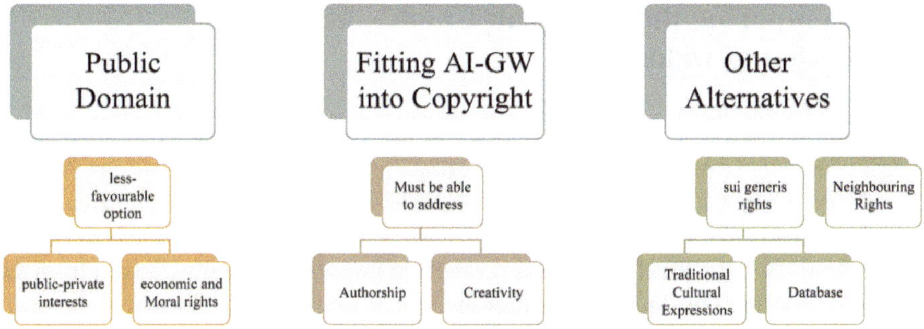

Fig. 1.1 Copyright law's options in accommodating AI-generated works *Source* The author

multiple parties performing different roles. Moreover, the creation and use of AI-generated works in Indonesia involves both public and private interests that require protection. Further, contributors of AI-generated works may desire ownership in order to protect their investment in the works.

The second option is to fit AI-generated works into the existing framework of copyright law in some manner. As discussed in the previous section, this option is difficult given the legal interpretations of the authorship and creativity requirements of copyright law, since both concepts require direct human involvement.

I then turn to exploring the third option, that is, protecting AI-generated works with other proprietary rights available within copyright law, namely, *sui generis* right and neighbouring rights. I discuss the possibility of using both *sui generis* rights: a mechanism that has been widely used for protecting intangible heritage and database rights. In doing so, I look at how these two *sui generis* rights have been constructed and deployed across different jurisdictions, including Indonesia. This analysis provides me with appropriate *sui generis* models that either fit existing Indonesian legal structures, as is the case for the *sui generis* model I explore pertaining to the regulation of intangible heritage, or are specifically focused on computing technologies, as is the case concerning the *sui generis* model pertaining to database rights. However, as the nature of their objects of protection differ somewhat from those of AI-generated works, this study asserts that these two models for *sui generis* rights do offer suitable protection.

I offer instead an alternative option by noting that AI-generated works present interesting similarities to sound recordings and broadcasts, objects that do not attract copyright, but are protected by neighbouring rights. Recordings and broadcasts are often addressed differently across jurisdictions. For example, in Australia and the United Kingdom, they are described as subject matter other than works, and in the EU as auxiliaries of creations, while in Indonesia they are called related right products. See the footnotes for a note on terminology.[38]

[38] ***A note on terminology:*** One of the challenges created by AI-generated subject matter relates to how it should be classified. For example, whether it should be referred to as a potential new authorial work, or as a subject matter other than works (or neighbouring rights). These problems

1.4 Comparing the European Union's Approach to that of Indonesia

The primary reason why this book looks at the EU approach to generative AI is because the EU is one of the first jurisdictions to regulate AI. Through its AI Act, the EU shows that it has been ahead of Indonesia and many other countries in the world. Additionally, this book is looking at the EU's copyright approach to protect AI-generated works. **First,** Indonesian copyright law was originally derived from the Dutch's copyright law. During and after the Dutch's colonial era, Indonesia receives much influence from the European-continental copyright system, and hence, its copyright has some similarities. One of the most apparent similarities between Indonesia and the EU Member States is the acknowledgement of moral rights. These countries are known for their strong recognition of moral rights, as opposed to countries like the US, Singapore, and China, whose scope of moral rights is quite limited and may be waived.[39] Another similarity in both Indonesia and EU Member States is that in establishing one's authorship, they require a reflection of the author's personality into the work.[40] During the romantic author period, as discussed in Chap. 5 of this book, meeting the requirement of personality was relatively straightforward, as authors produced their work through their own intellectual efforts. However, as technology develops, the personality requirement becomes more challenging to meet for works created of machines or computer programs.

Second, EU's attempt in regulating AI has little to no stipulations on copyright and generative AI. It shows that despite EU's attempt to regulate AI, there are some aspects of it that needs to be discussed further. Similarly, Indonesia also has yet to update its copyright law in responding to the development of generative AI. Both of these jurisdictions need internal regulations as well as an internationally-harmonised ones because, more often than not, the operation of generative AI transcends national jurisdiction. A harmonisation attempt among EU Member States have been proven challenging, let alone to have an internationally-harmonised rules in governing ownership of AI-generated works. Due to these two similarities, it is possible that Indonesia and EU may have similar approach in responding to the questions brought by AI-generated works.

---

are compounded by the fact that the language used in Indonesian intellectual property law does not map directly onto the European-based terminology. To avoid confusion, this book refers to AI-generated subject matter as AI-generated works.

[39] Wan 2011, p. 465.

[40] Rosati 2013, pp. 63–64.

1.5 Why a Focus on the Indonesian Context?

Indonesia represents an interesting site for exploring this research topic for four reasons. **First**, Indonesia has identified the development and use of generative AI as a national strategic goal, particularly across five priority sectors, such as health, bureaucracy reform, smart city, education, and food security. One of the goals set in the National Strategy for Artificial Intelligence 2020-2045 (i.e., the "National Strategy") is to use generative AI systems in supporting those top five priorities.[41] It is anticipated that this strategy will increase the use of generative AI systems and the production of AI-generated works in Indonesia. Clarifying the question of copyright in this context will help to provide legal certainty for parties involved in creating AI-generated works. Additionally, given that the production and use of generative AI is often internationally distributed, there are increasing pressures to reconcile the international legal heterogeneity regulating such sophisticated computing technology.[42] This pressure extends to questions of copyright in AI-generated works given that the necessary software, underlying training data, and the distribution of the resulting work can involve numerous parties from different jurisdictions. Internationally harmonised norms may assist in regulating these relationships, and the resulting creative works, in a legally transparent, and predictable manner.[43]

Second, existing literature in this space tends to focus on European and the United States' law, with little attention paid to middle-income or low-income countries. However, like many middle-income countries around the world, Indonesia has different domestic priorities and has been subject to different international pressures that have historically impacted upon how copyright law operates. By locating my research in Indonesia, I seek to both destabilise the international techno-imaginary of Asian countries as pirate nations, and emphasise these countries as locations of creative labour on their own terms.

Third, Indonesia has historically deployed copyright law experimentally to foster public welfare and socio-economic development. For example, shortly after Independence, President Soekarno abolished copyright protection for foreign works to ensure Indonesians could freely access educational and cultural materials, a move that quite possibly envisaged the global information commons movement of the 1990s

---

[41] In 2020, Indonesia's Agency of Assessment and Application of Technology (*Badan Pengkajian dan Penerapan Teknologi* or "BPPT") published Indonesia's AI development plan in the National Strategy of Artificial Intelligence 2020–2045.

[42] Frohlich 2009, p. 852.

[43] As Hugenholtz asserts, the harmonised legal rule may enhance 'legal certainty, transparency, and predictability of norms' in copyright (Hugenholtz 2013, p. 65). For instance, when the production of AI-generated works involves creators from the United States and the United Kingdom, where the former rejects copyright of AI-generated works and the latter gives the protection of AI-generated works to anyone who has made the 'arrangement necessary' to the work, there may be confusion as to whether rights exist and, if so, who might own these and how they might be enforced. Given that the production of AI-generated works is accelerating and some of these works are attracting substantial value, this confusion calls for an internationally unified response to ensure legal certainty for all the parties involved in the production of AI-generated works.

and 2000s generally, and the position of the global South copyleft activists specifically.[44] In another experimental use of copyright law, the Indonesian legislature developed *sui generis* mechanisms to recognise the rights of indigenous communities (albeit regarding cultural heritage objects),[45] possibly providing a similar template for recognising multiple authorship in AI-generated works.[46]

Fourth, Indonesia has historically been considered to be a 'pirate' nation with substandard copyright enforcement. As a consequence, the development of Indonesian copyright law has, over the decades, been subject to significant international trading pressures - often at the expense of local creative and technological industries. Despite this, Indonesia has a vibrant and growing information technology sector. In 2022, Indonesia attracted 25% of private funding among countries in South-East Asia to develop its digital technology. Within the first six months of 2002, its digital sector attracted USD1,500,000,000 foreign investment.[47] Indonesia becomes an attractive investment destination for giant technology company because it has a massive number of technology users, as high as 213 million people, or 77% of the country's population. Specifically, AI users in Indonesia has currently reached 45% of its population.[48] As such, its copyright law must and should reflect the interests of local industry and people. In this sense, Indonesia has a vested interest in consciously shaping both domestic and global copyright law.

As a middle-income country, Indonesia can and should influence the development of global intellectual property policy. History shows examples of how middle-income countries have disrupted global intellectual property policy by requesting exceptions to ensure that their national interests and priorities are met. In the scope of global copyright policy, India, Brazil, Mexico and Portugal played important roles in representing middle-income countries' interests by demanding exemptions from international copyright law.[49] These countries, along with other middle-income countries, requested that global copyright policy take into account the 'divergent economic, social, cultural, and technological conditions in the developing world'.[50] The ensuing proposal led to the 1967 Stockholm Revision of the Berne Convention Protocol regarding Developing Countries (the Stockholm Revision) being established. The Stockholm Provision ensures that developing countries can, for a limited period of

[44] Kusumadara 2000.

[45] Kariodimedjo 2019.

[46] The attempt to provide *sui generis* protection for the traditional cultural expression was started in 2008 through the Draft of Act on The Protection of Traditional Knowledge and Traditional Cultural Expressions (RUU PTEBT). Unfortunately, to this date, the draft has not been enacted into law. A similar Act was enacted in 2017 on Cultural Advancement which allows local communities to make an inventory, safeguard, and preserve cultural objects. Yet this law does not regulate the granting of proprietary rights to either single or multiple authors, see Kusumadara 2011.

[47] Catriana and Pratama 2022.

[48] Annur 2023.

[49] WIPO 1967.

[50] Yu 2009.

time, allowed for domestic copyright laws that offer more relaxed protections than the international standard.[51]

As a middle-income country in the South-East Asian region, Indonesia also takes part in transforming global intellectual property policy. In 1958, Indonesia withdrew its membership from the Berne Convention to ensure that copyright-protected educational resources, such as textbooks, which were comparatively costly in that country, could be circulated freely. This aspiration, to ensure that middle income countries could access protected works for educational purposes, was later accommodated in Article 1 (e) of Stockholm Revision.[52] Although, as a result of its withdrawal from the Berne Convention, Indonesia did not directly participate in the Stockholm Conference, the state did participate in the East Asian Seminar on Copyright in New Delhi which took place five months earlier. The East Asian Seminar adopted resolutions requiring a lower standard of copyright protection for developing countries, which became the basis for the developing countries' proposal in the Stockholm Revision.[53]

Indonesia's involvement in the global protection of intellectual property is not restricted to copyright law. Indonesia has been actively involved in protecting traditional knowledge[54] and traditional cultural expressions. For example, Indonesia sponsored a written request that was later introduced as Article 29*bis* in the Agreement on Trade-Related Aspects of Intellectual Property Rights (TRIPs agreement), which requires the member States of the World Trade Organization (WTO) to disclose the source of origin of the biological resources and traditional knowledge in patent applications.[55] This disclosure is important to prevent patents over genetic resources and traditional knowledge that lack novelty and an inventive step. Additionally, the disclosure requirement also helps to prevent traditional knowledge from being exploited without fair and equitable benefit sharing.

---

[51] The Stockholm Protocol gives developing countries rights to reservation to some articles of the Berne Conventions so that the developing countries could address their own concerns over access and development.

[52] Article 1 (e) of the Stockholm Revision mentions that any developing country, for the first ten years after ratification of the Convention, may enjoy reservations to "reserve the right, exclusively for teaching, study, and research in all fields of education, to restrict the protection of literary and artistic works, provided due provision shall be made by domestic legislation to assure to the author a compensation which conforms to standards of payment made to national authors [...]".

[53] Yu 2009.

[54] Traditional knowledge includes the "know-how, skills, innovations, practices, and learning that form part of traditional knowledge systems, and knowledge that is embodied in the traditional lifestyle of a community or people, or is contained in codified knowledge systems passed between generations. It is not limited to any technical field, and may include agricultural, environmental, and medicinal knowledge, and knowledge associated with genetic resources." See *World Intellectual Property Organization, Consultation Paper: Recommendations on the Recognition of Traditional Knowledge in the Patent System* (Intergovernmental Communication on Intellectual Property and Genetic Resources, Traditional Knowledge, and Folklore No WIPO/GRTKF/IC/13/7).

[55] *Draft Decision to Enhance Mutual Supportiveness between the TRIPs Agreement and the Convention of Biological Diversity (World Trade Organization)* (Communication from Brazil, China, Colombia, Ecuador, India Indonesia, Peru, Thailand, the ACP Group and the African Group No TN/C/W/59).

Indonesia's position in developing global intellectual property protection exemplifies how a middle-income country might intervene, either independently or with a larger bloc of similarly situated states, to shape international copyright law according to its own needs, interests and priorities. Those needs may destabilise the existing one-size-fits-all global intellectual property regulation whose formation has been primarily influenced by high-income countries. Such conditions drive middle-income countries to participate in and influence the development of global IP regulation so that their needs and interests are accommodated. However, Indonesia cannot make such a useful intervention into global IP law in relation to AI-generated works without a serious study of how these AI-generated works affect copyright law. This book supports Indonesia's position as a middle-income country's potential to not only shape appropriate domestic policy, but also points towards how Indonesia can contribute to improved global copyright law, specifically, as well as international intellectual property and technology laws, more generally.

References

Abbott R (2016) I Think, Therefore I Invent: Creative Computers and the Future of Patent Law. Boston College Law Review 57(4):1079–1126

Annur C M (2023) Survei: ChatGPT Jadi Aplikasi Ai Paling Banyak Digunakan di Indonesia [Survey: ChatGPT Becomes the Most Used AI Application in Indonesia]. katadata. https://databoks.katadata.co.id/infografik/2023/06/26/survei-chatgpt-jadi-aplikasi-ai-paling-banyak-digunakan-di-indonesia

Boyle J (2003) The Second Enclosure Movement And The Construction Of The Public Domain. Law and Contemporary Problems 66:33–74

Catriana E, Pratama A M (2022) Indonesia Jadi Negara yang Paling Dilirik Investor untuk Investasi Teknologi di Asia Tenggara [Indonesia Becomes the Most Attractive Country for Tech Investment in South-East Asia]. Kompas.com. https://money.kompas.com/read/2022/11/08/171000326/indonesia-jadi-negara-yang-paling-dilirik-investor-untuk-investasi-teknologi

Friedman D D (2001) Does technology require new law? Harvard Journal of Law and Public Policy 25(1):71–85

Frohlich A B (2009) Copyright Infringement in the Internet Age—Primetime for Harmonized Conflict-of-Laws Rules? Berkeley Technology Law Journal 24(2):851–896

Grant T D, Wischik D J (2020) On the path to AI. Springer Nature, Switzerland

Hugenholtz P B (2012) The story of The Tape Recorder and The History of Copyright Levies. In: Sherman B, Wiseman L (eds) Copyright and the Challenge of the New. Kluwer Law International, The Netherlands, pp 179–196

Hugenholtz P B (2013) Is harmonization a good thing? The case of the copyright acquis. In: Pila J, Ohly A (eds) The Europeanization of intellectual property law: towards a European legal methodology. Oxford University Press, Oxford, pp 57–74. https://doi.org/10.1093/acprof:oso/9780199665105.003.0004

Hugenholtz P B, Quintais J P (2021) Copyright and Artificial Creation: Does EU Copyright Law Protect AI-Assisted Output? IIC - International Review of Intellectual Property and Competition Law 52(9):1190–1216. https://doi.org/10.1007/s40319-021-01115-0

Huson G (2018) I, Copyright. Santa Clara High Technology Law Journal 35(2):54–78

Kariodimedjo D W (2019) Illuminating the Future by Safeguarding and Protecting Intangible Cultural Heritage in Indonesia. Doctor of Philosophy Thesis, Charles Darwin University, Australia

Kusumadara A (2000) Analysis of the Failure of the Implementation of Intellectual Property Laws in Indonesia. Doctor of Philosophy Thesis, University of Sydney. http://hdl.handle.net/2123/820

Kusumadara A (2011) Pemeliharaan dan pelestarian pengetahuan tradisional dan ekspresi budaya tradisional Indonesia: Perlindungan hak kekayaan intelektual dan non-hak kekayaan intelektual [T. Jurnal Hukum Ius Quia Iustum 18(1):20–41. https://doi.org/10.20885/iustum.vol18.iss1.art2

Kwall R R (2006) Inspiration and innovation: The intrinsic dimension of the artistic soul. Notre Dame L. Rev. 81(5):1945–2012

Lessig L (2001) The Future of Ideas: The Fate of The Commons in a Connected World. Vintage Books, New York

Lim D (2018) AI & IP: Innovation & Creativity in an Age of Accelerated Change. Akron Law Review 52:813–875

Moses L B (2003) Adapting the law to technological change: a comparison of common law and legislation. University of New South Wales law journal 26(2):394–417

Perry M, Margoni T (2010) From music tracks to Google maps: Who owns computer-generated works? Computer Law & Security Review 26(6):621–629. https://doi.org/10.1016/j.clsr.2010.09.005

Popelier P (2017) Legal certainty and the European courts: accessibility and legitimate expectations as standards of reasonableness. In: Fenwick M (ed) The shifting meaning of legal certainty in comparative and transnational law. Hart Publishing, Oxford, pp 29–54

Quackenbush C (2018) A Painting Made by Artificial Intelligence Has Been Sold at Auction for $432,500. Time. https://time.com/5435683/artificial-intelligence-painting-christies/. Accessed 6 February 2020

Rosati E (2013) Originality in EU Copyright: Full Harmonization through Case Law, 1st edn. Edward Elgar Publishing, Cheltenham

Samuelson P (1986) Allocating Ownership Rights in Computer-Generated Works. University of Pittsburgh Law Review 47:1185–1228

Schaumann N (1983) Copyright Protection in the Cable Television Industry: Satellite Retransmission and the Passive Carrier Exemption. Fordham Law Review 51(4):637–665

Sherman B, Wiseman L (eds) (2012) Copyright and the challenge of the new. Kluwer Law International B.V., The Netherlands

Swire P (2008) Consumers as Producers. The Internet and the Future of Consumer Protection, 24 July 2006

Ventimiglia A (2020) The Angel in the Machine: Divining Legal Authorship in Channelled and Computer-Generated Works. In: Voss E (ed) Mediality on Trial: Testing and Contesting Trance and Other Media Techniques. De Gruyter Oldenbourg, Berlin/Boston, pp 236–260. https://doi.org/10.1515/9783110416411-009

Wan Y (2011) Moral rights of authors in China. Journal of the Copyright Society of the U.S.A. 58(2):455–481

White C, Matulionyte R (2020) Artificial Intelligence Painting The Bigger Picture For Copyright Ownership. Australian Intellectual Property Journal 30:181–247

World Intellectual Property Organization (WIPO) (1967) Records of the Intellectual Property Conference of Stockholm, June 11 to July 14, 1967, Volume 2. World Intellectual Property Organization, Geneva

Yanisky-Ravid S, Velez-Hernandez L A (2018) Copyrightability of Artworks Produced by Creative Robots and Originality: The Formality-Objective Model. Minnesota Journal of Law, Science and Technology 19(1):1–53

Yu P K (2009) A Tale of Two Development Agendas. Ohio Northern University Law Review 35:465–573

Yu R (2017) The machine author: what level of copyright protection is appropriate for fully independent computer-generated works? University of Pennsylvania Law Review 165(5):1245–1270

Zimmerman D L (2011) Copyrights as Incentives: Did We Just Imagine That? Theoretical Inquiries in Law 12(1):29–58

Chapter 2
Background Information on Indonesian Copyright Law and Generative AI

Contents

Abstract The shaping of Indonesian copyright law into its current form has been influenced by both external and internal factors. Initially, it was heavily influenced by Dutch law during its early years of independence. Later, Indonesia faced international pressures from the US and the UK due to its failure to meet international copyright protection standards. Domestically, copyright in Indonesia is a complex domain because it has to accommodate both *adat* (customary) and Islamic law. With the rapid development of technology, Indonesian copyright law must evolve while reflecting the socio-technical realities of its people. When dealing with AI specifically, Indonesia has a National Strategy on AI which focuses on five priority sectors, namely education, health, bureaucracy reform, food security, and smart cities. While this strategy outlines the general objectives for AI, it does not address the ownership of AI-generated works. The discussion in this chapter also explores the technological aspects of generative AI, emphasising the importance of the human contribution in creating AI-generated works.

Keywords Indonesian copyright law · TRIPs · Modern copyright law · Indonesian copyright history · Artificial intelligence · Machine learning · AI-generated works · Generative AI · National Strategy on Artificial Intelligence

L. Andrini, *Protecting Artificial Intelligence-generated Works in Indonesia*, Information Technology and Law Series 41, https://doi.org/10.1007/978-94-6265-703-8_2

2.1 Introduction

One of the challenges that arises in discussing copyright protection for AI-generated works is that while copyright is administered locally in accordance with national jurisdictions, the operation of generative AI systems often extend across national borders. To date, Indonesia does not offer copyright protection for AI-generated works. Other jurisdictions, such as the United States and the United Kingdom, however, have already set conditions where AI-generated works may be protected: notably, when there is human contribution to the works. Different rules of protection for AI-generated works across nation-states increases the chance that works produced by the same generative AI system may be protected in one state, but not in others. In the first part of this chapter, I look at the possibility of protecting AI-generated works through Indonesia's perspectives by looking at how Indonesian copyright law has been influenced by colonial rules, shaped by international pressures, and its own customary (*adat*) law.

The second part of this chapter introduces frequently-used forms of terminology associated with AI-generated works to provide an easier understanding of the discussions in the following chapters. It also describes the steps generally involved in creating AI-generated outputs – only a portion of which might mimic human creativity and, therefore, give rise to AI-generated works. Each of these steps identifies what humans contribute to the process of creating an AI-generated work. Exploring the technical components required to produce AI-generated works through the operation of generative AI is essential to determine whether, and how, copyright or other proprietary rights should be allocated.

2.2 The Relevance of Indonesia's Copyright Law to a Broader Audience

The discussion of copyright protection in Indonesia is relevant not only for scholars in Indonesia, but also for audiences from other jurisdictions. Even though intellectual property is generally administered nationally, intangible assets, such as AI systems and their outputs, have historically moved easily across state borders. As a result, numerous international agreements have been developed to harmonise laws pertaining to these cross-boundary objects, such as the Berne Convention for the Protection of Literary and Artistic Works (1886) and the Paris Convention for the Protection of Industrial Property (1883). These agreements, which continue today, provide minimum proprietary protections for intangible properties.[1] The importance of these agreements has accelerated in the computing age when exploiting intellectual property is easier than before.[2] In this situation, what happens in Indonesia may

[1] Lessig 2001.

[2] For example, songs can now be enjoyed through digital platforms that do not require the movement of physical goods such as VCDs or DVDs.

have implications for other jurisdictions. This is especially true because, since Independence Indonesia has viewed copyright as a tool to improve access to education, health, and infrastructure. This approach may produce different policies surrounding how copyright protection develops and changes.[3]

Within Indonesia, the following factors contribute to the country's individual approach to protecting intellectual property, generally, and copyright, specifically:

- The role of international law and market forces in structuring the domestic regulation of intellectual property in southeast Asian countries that presents the region as the site of 'tradition' and/or 'piracy' but not as modern 'creativity';
- The ways in which legal change proceeds in Indonesia, a country whose legal system is marked by its Dutch colonial heritage, Islamic law, and *adat.*

2.2.1 Reconfiguring Indonesia: From Site of Tradition and Piracy to Site of Creative Activity

Indonesian copyright law has historically been shaped by other jurisdictions: firstly, by foreign colonial influences and later by international pressures because of the country's reputation as a pirate nation. Chief among these influences is Dutch copyright law, from which modern Indonesian copyright directly descends from colonisation. Upon Independence in 17 August 1945, Indonesia inherited its Dutch colonial membership to the Berne Convention. While enforcement of Indonesia's copyright law had been domestically suspended in the immediate post-Independence era, the country's first president, Soekarno, formally withdrew from the state's obligations under the Berne Convention in 1958. Soekarno is recorded as making this decision to ensure that education materials could be made widely and publicly available.[4] Indonesia's re-entry into the Berne Convention in 1997 resulted from its participation in the Uruguay Round.[5]

By the 1980s, and possibly before, Indonesia had a reputation as pirate market owing to the massive piracy of foreign works such as phonogram recordings.[6]

---

[3] A relevant example on how countries with developing economies may treat IPs differently can be found in the landmark Novartis case that took place in India. India is considered the third largest pharmaceutical producer in the world. One of the drugs produced by generic producers in India is Glivec, a medicine useful in the treatment of cancer by stalling its development. Glivec's patent holder, Novartis, had attempted to register for patent protection of Glivec in India. However, in 2006 such application was rejected on the grounds that it 'did not demonstrate any significant changes in therapeutic effectiveness over its pre-existing form, which was already patented outside India.' In a response to this, Novartis filed a lawsuit to the Madras High Court to question the compliance of Section 3(d) of the Indian Patents Act to TRIPs. As the High Court overturned Novartis' claim, it filed the lawsuit to the Indian Supreme Court – who also decided against Novartis on the grounds of public health safeguards in TRIPs, as the court wanted to guarantee the population's affordable access to medicine (Gabble and Kohler 2014, p. 1).

[4] Kusumadara 2000, p. 38.

[5] Drahos 1996a, pp. 57–58.

[6] Lepp 1990 at 28 in Kusumadara 2000.

Some European and North American countries, who suffered losses from this piracy happening in Indonesia threatened to abolish Indonesia's trade preferential treatment if it failed to improve its copyright protection for foreign works.[7] This pressure led Indonesia to participate in the Uruguay Round, a multilateral negotiation under the General Agreement on Tariffs and Trade (GATT).[8] In this round, Indonesia discussed intellectual property rights, trade-related investment measures, anti-dumping, sanitary and phytosanitary measures, technical barrier to trade, and related issues.[9] Another important milestone reached by the Uruguay Round was the establishment of the World Trade Organization.[10] With regards to intellectual property, the round resulted in the Trade Related Aspects of Intellectual Property (TRIPs) Agreement, a measure championed by the United States to provide substantive standards, enforcement, and dispute settlement regarding trade-related intellectual property.[11] The TRIPs Agreement also stipulates that Member States comply with existing international conventions on the protection of IP including: the Paris Convention on the Protection of Industrial Property (Paris Convention) and the Berne Convention for the Protection of Literary and Artistic Works (Berne Convention).[12] As a member to the TRIPs Agreement, Indonesia is obligated to comply with these international conventions.

The TRIPs Agreement recognises the principle of *national treatment* which provides that:

> Each Member shall accord to the nationals of other Members treatment no less favourable than it accords to its own nationals with regard to the protection of intellectual property, subject to the exceptions already provided in, respectively, the Paris Convention (1967), the Berne Convention (1971), the Rome Convention on the Treaty on Intellectual Property in Respect of Integrated Circuits.

The principle of national treatment requires Member States to provide the nationals of other Member States with treatment *"no less favourable than"* the protection given to its own nationals. This means that without national legal framework which protects AI-generated works in Indonesia, it cannot protect similar works coming from other countries.

At present, Indonesia has not adopted any measures or clarified the copyright protection associated with AI-generated works. Meanwhile, some other countries have explicitly accommodated AI-generated works in their national legislation. The legal frameworks in countries like the United Kingdom, New Zealand, Ireland, Hong

[7] Kusumadara 2000, p. 160.

[8] GATT was established in 1947 during the Geneva Round with the main purpose of trade liberalisation. Since its establishment, its members have met and negotiated in multiple rounds, each having an agenda to promote trade liberalisation and reduce trade barriers.

[9] Preeg 2012.

[10] Ibid.

[11] Bello and Holmer 1990.

[12] Article 1.2., *Agreement on Trade-Related Aspects of Intellectual Property Rights, opened for signature 15 April 1994 (entered into force 1 January 1995)* (TRIPs Agreement).

Kong, and South Africa grant authorship to the person who performs the "arrangements necessary" in creating the work.[13] Similarly, India's Copyright Act recognises that the author of AI-generated works shall be "the person who cause the work to be created."[14] Under the TRIPs' national treatment obligation, countries are required to protect AI-generated works created within other member States of TRIPs agreement. However, problems may arise when AI-generated works from those countries are used in other countries with lower protection, such as Indonesia.[15] The National Treatment principle cannot compel Indonesia to provide protection to AI-generated works as its national legal framework does not even protect such works created by its nationals. Consequently, the AI-generated works coming from those other countries may not be protected under Indonesian copyright law and may be used without risk of infringement.

Differences in national legislations may create conflicts when AI-generated works are used without permission in non-protective jurisdictions. When this happens, international obligations such as the national treatment under TRIPs agreement, may not suffice to resolve the problems. Thus, regulation at the national level is needed to protect domestic and foreign works.

2.2.2 *The Imprint of Plural Legal Traditions on Indonesian Copyright Law: Challenges and Opportunities for Thinking Creatively About the Regulation of AI-generated Works*

Indonesian law is shaped by its history as a plural legal system that combines Dutch colonial law, *adat* law, and Islamic law. The interaction of these legal traditions has not been without problems. For example, regarding private property, Dutch law emphasises the idea of individual ownership while most *adat* laws and Islamic law, especially pertaining to inheritance, stress communal management and familial maintenance obligations, respectively.[16] Consequently, when it comes to protecting intellectual property, inevitable mismatches exist in these legal traditions. From a socio-legal perspective, there is often a tension between *adat* law's emphasis on the notion of communal property and Dutch law's emphasis on the discrete individual person – something that is particularly emphasized in the Dutch interpretation of copyright that informs Indonesian law in this space. This tension between a colonial legal transplant and Indonesian social norms has contributed to patterns of piracy in consumer consumption of copyrighted works – a pattern that reached its peak in the 1980s and 1990s. At the same time, attempts to address and better regulate piracy,

---

[13] McCutcheon 2012, pp. 956–957.

[14] McCutcheon 2012.

[15] Taking into account that most works, including AI-generated works, can be distributed across national borders easily due to the presence of internet connections.

[16] Butt 2002.

which led to the overhaul of Indonesian copyright legislation in the 1980s, failed to generate a general awareness of intellectual property.

The broad unrestrained piracy described above leads to the problematic result of a foreign legal transplant (modern copyright law) into Indonesia's plural legal system.[17] Simon Butt asserts that the absence of a popular legal consciousness regarding copyright during the 1980s – 1990s occurred because most Indonesians, both as creators and consumers of protected content, did not enjoy the benefits of copyright.[18] Indeed, Butt argues that copyright protections in Indonesia primarily functioned to benefit foreign entities.[19] From the 1980s to the present, most copyright-protected works in Indonesia were produced by foreign authors located in developed countries, such as the United States and Europe.[20] Therefore, establishing and enforcing copyright protection in Indonesia is believed to provide more benefit to foreigners from the developed world than to local peoples, businesses, or other entities.

Despite the framing of copyright as a problematic legal transplant, Indonesian regulation has been increasingly shaped to accommodate the interests of local communities in creative ways. Such attempts at experimenting with the law may prove useful in considering the regulation of AI-generated works which are, themselves, novel types of work produced by stakeholders in roles not typically associated with copyright. For example, the 2014 amendments to the Copyright Act recognised traditional cultural expressions (TCE)[21] as a new object of protection. In so doing, the amendment recognises that traditional cultural expressions were produced by numerous, and often anonymous, creators occupying different roles in the production process. However, the revisions pertaining to such communal interests outlined in the 2014 Copyright Act still face criticism as it gives the copyright of communally authored cultural expressions to the State, not the local community.[22] While traditional cultural expressions and AI-generated works might at first seem to be contradictory, they are both produced similarly involving numerous, often anonymous, stakeholders. They occupy different roles that might contribute layer upon layer in such a way that discerning their influences on the final product is difficult. In this sense, traditional cultural expressions and AI-generated works may share common

[17] See Saidin 2016; Bedner 2013.

[18] Butt 2002.

[19] Ibid.

[20] Works like movies, songs, and computer programs in Indonesia are generally imported from developed countries. In 2018 alone, Hollywood's box office movies made a profit estimated at USD 355 million from Indonesian market (Sarahtika 2019).

[21] Traditional cultural expressions shall mean intellectual works in the field of art, including literal expression which contains elements of characteristics from traditional heritage which are produced, developed, and maintained by a particular community or society. This includes verbal-textual, musical, motion, theatre, fine art, as well as *adat* ceremony. The definition and classification can be found in the Draft of Act on the Protection and Utilization of Intellectual Property of Traditional Knowledge and Traditional Cultural Expressions.

[22] Granting copyright of traditional cultural expressions to the state may jeopardize the community's rights as they cannot control/utilise the Traditional cultural expressions on their own, see Article 38(1), *Law number 28 of 2014 on Copyright 2014 (Indonesia)* (2014 Copyright Act).

features that challenge core concepts of Indonesian copyright law including the idea that the work reflects elements of the author's personality. Thus, attempts to resolve a similar issue in Indonesian copyright law, such as numerous and anonymous authorial inputs, may provide an instructive model for other types of work. In the case of traditional cultural expressions, legislative reforms suggest it is suitable to assign ownership rights, not with local communities or creators, but with the state as a type of guardianship role. This suggests that a creative solution for AI-generated works might involve a similar corporate entity that represents the different people involved in creating the work, such as a collecting society or some new public or private organisational form.

In most cases, Indonesian creators, whether individual authors, corporate employers, or local communities producing cultural expressions, increasingly desire copyright protection to ensure that they acquire the benefits resulting from the commercialisation of their work.[23] This demonstrates a growing legal consciousness of the importance of copyright protection among creative workers, as they want the law to be applied and enforced to protect their interests. In this sense, despite a domestic copyright regime that has historically been shaped and influenced by international pressure, Indonesian law has moved to accommodate its own domestic agenda and interests. In other words, copyright law, once considered a problematic legal transplant, has been reconceptualised and reconfigured by many domestic stakeholders as a means to adequately protect their own interests.

2.2.3 Indonesia Today: National Reliance on Information Technology

Increased meaningful access to information technology is significant in Indonesia's economic growth.[24] AI marks one of the expanding information technology sectors presumed to benefit both the public and private sectors in Indonesia. In the private sector, AI has been developed by corporations to support businesses' automation and efficiency, business analysis and findings, consumer-based recommendations, and fraud detection and security. To date, generative AI has mainly been used to facilitate content generation and creative collaboration with human authors. The number of companies running generative AI in Indonesia is comparatively smaller than its neighbouring country, Singapore. Nonetheless, given that AI keeps on gaining traction, more supply and demand of generative AI is predicted.

Besides a growing private interest in developing generative AI, the Indonesian government has envisaged using generative AI to support public interests.

[23] In 2015, Indonesian book authors, publishers, song writers, singers, recording companies, and filmmakers did campaign against piracy with the tagline "*Stop Pembajakan!*" (Stop Piracy!) as many of their works were pirated into VCDs or made available online for free (Setiawan 2015).

[24] It was reported that the information technology sector contributed 4,5% to the growth of Indonesia's gross domestic product (GDP) in 2020 (Damuri and Fauri 2021).

This is reflected in Indonesia's National Strategy Plan for Artificial Intelligence, published by Indonesia's Agency of Assessment and Application of Technology (*Badan Pengkajian dan Penerapan Teknologi* or "BPPT") in August 2020.[25] This strategy establishes five priorities for AI development in Indonesia, namely: health, bureaucracy reform, education, food security, as well as mobility and smart cities.[26] Of these priorities the following two are particularly relevant when discussing the issue of how copyright law would be applied to AI-generated works. First, in the education sector, the National Strategy projects that universities, schools, and private actors (software companies) will be involved in producing AI-generated works to improve student learning in the form of multimedia content and games.[27] Regarding mobility and smart city applications, the National Strategy compels Indonesia to create AI-generated maps for use in developing better mobility plans, smart city applications, and disaster management plans.[28] This effort will involve regional government entities, the Ministry of Communication and Information, universities and private parties.[29]

In addition to these policies, Indonesia also has a growing creative industry which is increasingly adopting AI tools to support its development. Although not mentioned in the priorities of AI national development, this industry is another sector to look at for two reasons. First, it has added significantly to Indonesia's GDP by 7% to its national GDP in 2017.[30] This contribution had increased to 12% in 2019.[31] Second, because AI-generated works have been widely used to support creative industries around the world, it seems that it can be used to support Indonesia's as well, as happens with the AI-generated work made by Microsoft Indonesia's AI in collaboration with the Indonesian designer Ria Miranda.[32,33]

The emphasis on using generative AI to develop AI-generated works in the National Strategy raises questions about applying copyright in those works. This calls for further discussion, especially regarding possible issues for copyright, such as authorial identity and personality, locations of creative work, and training data. Concerning authorship, the discussion should include whether an AI-generated work is a product of human or machine 'creativity'. Moreover, since producing AI-generated works usually involves more than one individual, addressing question of who should be deemed as the author of the work is also important. Another topic that needs to be addressed is how copyright law should treat training data. AI-generated

---

[25] Strategi Nasional Kecerdasan Artifisial, Badan Pengkajian dan Penerapan Teknologi (BPPT) 2020.

[26] Ibid.

[27] Ibid.

[28] Ibid. p. 184.

[29] Ibid.

[30] Singgih 2017.

[31] Ibid.

[32] Lukman 2019.

[33] Pictures, videos, audio recordings, games (computer programs), as well as maps are objects of copyright protection as set out in Article 40 of the 2014 Copyright Act, above n. 22.

works depend heavily on data given to the algorithm because this data is the main 'learning material' in generative AI.[34] As well, some of the data used to produce AI-generated works may be copyright-protected that begs the question about whether using such material as training data amounts to infringement or whether this would be exempted under fair-use doctrine.[35]

2.3 Background Information on Artificial Intelligence and AI-generated Works

2.3.1 Artificial Intelligence and Generative AI

Artificial intelligence (AI) is at the cutting edge of techno-scientific development. The inception of the field can be traced to the mid-twentieth century. The first mention of AI appeared in the Darthmouth Conference on intelligent behaviour in machines in 1956.[36] Marvin Minsky, one of the conference's organisers defined AI as 'the field of research concerned with making machines do things that people consider to require intelligence.[37] One revolutionary aspect of Minsky's framework was that it asserted that machines can perform complex tasks, in contrast to the popular belief at the time that they could accomplish only simple tasks:

> [M]ost people have a low opinion of the intellectual potentialities of machines. It is usually felt that although machines can be very fast, or very strong, they cannot be very smart. It is well known that machines have been made to do many things that meet high human standards... But it is usually felt that this reflects no credit on the machine that because the designer or programmer has set down every small detail of the process, the machine has only to perform (however quickly and accurately) simple clerical tasks.'[38]

AI was originally derived from work by scholars such as Alan Turing, who raised the possibility that a machine could be trained to be as intelligent as a human being.[39] More recently, AI has become 'a study of computer problems that have not yet been solved'.[40] This definition is believed to be more suitable to describe contemporary

[34] Surden 2014, p. 91.

[35] Discussions on whether using copyrighted data in the AI dataset is permitted can be found in Sobel 2018; Levendowski 2018; Lim 2018.

[36] The conference was organised by Marvin Minsky, John McCarthy, Nathanial Rochester, and Claude Shannon. Minsky was a Harvard junior fellow doing research in neural networks; he later founded the MIT AI laboratory; meanwhile McCarthy later founded the Stanford University AI Laboratory (Kurzweil and Jaroch 1990, pp. 198–199).

[37] Minsky 1986.

[38] Minsky 1967, p. 103.

[39] Turing introduced the Turing Test to show that a machine is intelligent enough when it interacts with a person, the person could not tell the difference whether the response was given by a human or a machine (Turing 1950; Bridy 2012).

[40] Kurzweil and Jaroch 1990.

work in AI since most machine-learning projects focus on developing programs in which the software, rather than the researcher, identifies and generates the output.

Since the 1950s, AI development has split into several branches that are distinguished by differing levels of complexity, with machine learning being at the more sophisticated edge of that spectrum. Specifically, the literature tends to divide AI capability into three areas, namely: 1) artificial narrow intelligence, 2) artificial general intelligence; and 3) superintelligence.[41] The discussion in this book focuses on artificial general intelligence as the type of AI software which that can perform complex tasks autonomously.[42] This research focuses on artificial general intelligence because of its autonomous nature in creating AI-generated works. Such autonomy does not exist in artificial narrow intelligence, while superintelligence is still currently being developed.

Generative AI relies mainly on machine learning algorithms - a branch of artificial intelligence used to detect patterns within data to predict future data.[43] Machine learning and its variation such as deep learning and large language models, can be used to create AI-generated works such as paintings, photographs, or books, which in some cases results in prize-winning works that generates substantial sales.[44]

2.3.2 The Process Involved in Creating AI-generated Works

Before describing how AI-generated works are created, it is important to understand some of technical terms used in the field. A computer program or software is 'a set of instructions that are expressed in the form of languages, codes, schemes, or in any form that is intended for a computer to perform specific functions or to achieve certain outcomes.'[45] Software has functions and interfaces that can be directly used by its users. Meanwhile, an algorithm is a procedure or formula to solve a problem. An algorithm needs to be written into a code so that it can be understood and executed by a computer program. The result of running the algorithm is called a model.[46]

Two of the machine learning models that are used to support generative AI are generative adversarial networks (GANs) and large language model (LLM). These machine learning models are capable of producing works by executing code from machine learning algorithm.[47] They can create new data from a set of learning data and enable software to generate new objects that may not have existed previously.

---

[41] Batin et al. 2017, p. 403.

[42] To date, superintelligence is a concept that is still far from its real-world application. Thus, it is not within the focus of this book to discuss superintelligence.

[43] Murphy 2012, p. 1.

[44] Statt 2017; Olewitz 2019.

[45] Article 1(9), 2014 Copyright Act, above n. 22.

[46] Interview data.

[47] The limitations of the deep neural networks (DNN) algorithm and the deep learning algorithm can be overcome by GAN. As an algorithm, DNN, which mimics how the human brain works, needs large sets of labelled data to work. This would require a lot of time and expense because it

Models adopted by generative AI software present a more advanced application than other branches of AI such as expert systems that imitate humans' decision-making ability, or fuzzy logic that helps decision cater for multiple criteria by assessing options.[48] To date, generative AI has been used to generate image datasets, human photographs, cartoon characters, and increase photo resolution.[49]

In general, creating AI-generated works involves three stages: determining software objectives, the learning process, and the production of works. Below I give brief descriptions of each of these three stages.

i) Determining software objectives
The first step of creating an AI-generated work is to determine its desired output. To do this, an objective for building the generative AI system needs to be determined and defined. An example of such an objective could be to build a generative AI system capable of producing images that appear to be photographs of human faces. There are at least two reasons why setting objectives is important at this stage. The first is that generative AI software is only capable of performing a specific objective; for example, when it is trained to convert text to an image. If properly structured, then that generative AI system software should not be able to do otherwise.[50] Secondly, having a specific objective at the initial stage of development helps to determine what kind of datasets are needed to train the generative AI software – an issue that arises at a later stage of system development. For example, if the objective is to generate human faces, then a data set containing a large and varied number of photographs containing human faces will be needed to train the system.[51]

ii) Learning process
In general, the learning process is understood as training the generative AI algorithm. This occurs when the system is provided with a set of training data from which the software can identify patterns from which it can be asked to generate new objects. The objective of a learning process is to train the algorithm to be able to 1) tell the difference between the 'real and 'fake' objects; and 2) generate the desired output. To achieve this purpose, a generative AI model needs two sub-models, namely *a generator* and *a discriminator*. A generator produces new objects resembling the training data, while a discriminator should be able to tell which objects are 'real' and belong to the training data and which are 'fake' and produced by the generator. See Fig. 2.1.

---

needs human operators to do the data-labelling. Meanwhile, deep learning does not need human operators to classify data, but it is not good at creating new data (objects). GAN exists to overcome the drawbacks of the previous two algorithms because it can classify data on its own, and later generate new sets of data (Dickson 2018).

[48] Singh et al. 2013.

[49] Brownlee 2019.

[50] Interview data.

[51] Ibid.

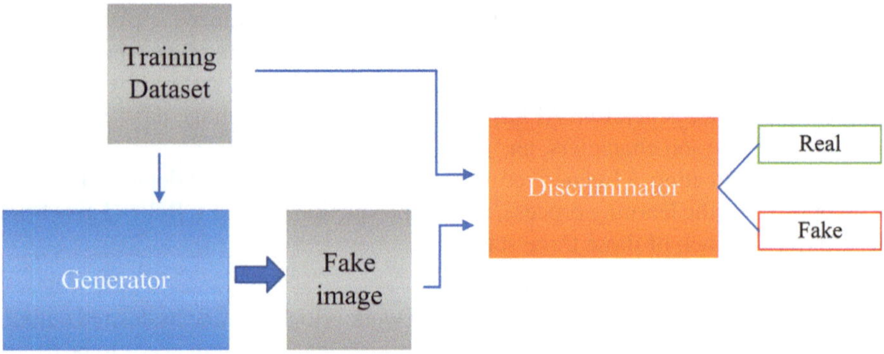

Fig. 2.1 Learning process of generative AI model *Source* The author

iii) Creation of AI-generated works
Once the interaction between the generator and discriminator has been optimised – in a way that the latter is finally not capable of telling whether the generated objects come from the real dataset or are created by the generator, the software is ready to produce AI-generated works.

It is important to note that the learning process involving a generator and discriminator is not one-sided or that it only proceeds in one direction. Instead, the interaction moves back and forth with the goal of 'fooling' the discriminator. A discriminator is a classifier that distinguishes real data from data created by a generator. If the discriminator is still able to tell that the objects are 'fake', then the generator needs to train itself so that the 'fake' objects are increasingly similar to the 'real' training data. The objective of this learning process is that the generator is able to create new objects in such a way that the discriminator would not be able to detect them as 'fake' anymore.

In a more-detailed explanation, David Lehr and Paul Ohm analyse the process of machine learning into two primary workflows: "playing with the data" and "the running model".[52] The former employs seven steps that programmers need to perform: problem definition, data collection, data cleaning, summary statistics review, data partitioning, model selection, and model training.[53] Meanwhile the running model represents the model deployment, where the algorithm makes decisions.[54] A simplified understanding of each process is described as follows:

a. Problem definition is the stage where programmers determine the objectives of the software: what it can do and how it functions to achieve a desirable result.
b. Data collection applies to a large amount of data that will later be used to train the software. The data can be collected by either the programmers or data analysts. It is also possible to buy data from providers.

---

[52] Lehr and Ohm 2017.

[53] Ibid., p. 655.

[54] Lehr and Ohm 2017.

c. Data cleaning is the stage where the already-collected data undergo a value correction. Lehr and Ohm explain that the data may have a missing or incorrect value. The purpose of data cleaning stage is to correct or find the true value, or otherwise delete the data to improve the relevancy and accuracy. This stage can be done by either programmers or data analysts.
d. Summary statistics review is the stage where the programmers/data analysts classify the data to weed out outliers,[55] that is, to eliminate values that fall far below or above markers line. They will usually classify the data and into several percentiles, and eliminates data which fall below 25th or above 75th markers.
e. Data partitioning entail programmers and/or data analysts separate the data into a 'training' dataset and a 'test' dataset. This stage seeks to improve the algorithm's accuracy later in the model training stage. First, the algorithm is given the training dataset to predict outcomes. Second, the outcomes are assessed using the test dataset to measure the accuracy of the algorithm.
f. Model selection requires the programmers/analysts to choose a kind, or class of the algorithm model to be implemented. This stage may result in one or several candidates of model to be trained in the next stage.
g. Model training happens when the programmers/analysts begin machine learning. First, the algorithm is given the training dataset to predict outcomes. Second, the outcomes are assessed using the test dataset to see how accurate the algorithm prediction can be. This is a repetitive process done to improve the accuracy of the algorithm's prediction.
h. Model deployment is the stage where the trained and ready algorithm, is turned into a 'running model.' This means that the programmers need to produce a more end-user friendly interface of the running model, as well as to make it capable of running continuously.[56]

In explaining the stages involved in the creation of AI-generated works, Lehr and Ohm also clarified misconceptions, namely that 1) generative AI workflows are not linear, but go back and forth to create better results; and that 2) generative AI involves the running model and additional steps that require contributions from programmers.[57]

Even though generative AI may be intelligent enough to generate works, these systems are not currently capable of operating independently and still require some human involvement. In their operation, there are at least three potential human contributors in creating AI-generated works: namely software developers, data analysts/data trainers, and software users. When data analysts/data trainers are not involved in creating generative AI, programmers typically work from the (1) problem definition stage up until the (8) model deployment stage. Meanwhile, when data analysts/trainers are involved, programmers contribute little to the (1) problem definition and (8) model deployment stages while the data trainers perform the (2) data

[55] Ibid., p. 683.

[56] By using 'capable of running continuously' Lehr and Ohm put the emphasis on the generative AI-software available online that has a large number of end-users.

[57] Lehr and Ohm 2017.

collection up to the (7) model training stages. After the model has been deployed, users can use it to produce AI-generated works. These role divisions between programmers, data analysts/trainers, and users are quite flexible, sometimes depend on the scale of production. In a smaller scale,[58] software developers can possibly perform all stages by themselves, while a bigger scale of production usually involves more people in the software development and deployment stage.

References

Batin M et al. (2017) Artificial Intelligence in Life Extension: from Deep Learning to Superintelligence. Informatica: An International Journal of Computing and Informatics 41(4):401–417

Bedner A (2013) Indonesian Legal Scholarship and Jurisprudence as an Obstacle for Transplanting Legal Institutions. Hague Journal on the Rule of Law 5:253–273. https://doi.org/10.1017/S1876404512001145

Bello J H, Holmer A F (1990) The GATT Uruguay Round: its significance for U.S. bilateral trade with Korea and Taiwan. Michigan Journal of International Law 11(2):307–325

Bridy A (2012) Coding Creativity: Copyright and the Artificially Intelligent Author. Stanford Technology Law Review 5:1–28

Brownlee J (2019) 18 Impressive Applications of Generative Adversarial Networks (GANs). Machine Learning Mastery. https://machinelearningmastery.com/impressive-applications-of-generative-adversarial-networks/. Accessed 3 February 2020

Butt S (2002) Intellectual property in Indonesia: a problematic legal transplant. EIPR: European Intellectual Property Review 24(9):249–437

Damuri Y R, Fauri A (2021) Potensi dan Kontribusi Sektor Digital terhadap Perekonomian Indonesia [The Potential and Contribution of the Digital Sector to Indonesia's Economy]. Centre for Strategic and International Studies, Jakarta

Dickson B (2018) What is GAN, the AI technique that makes computer creative? TechTalks https://bdtechtalks.com/2018/05/28/generative-adversarial-networks-artificial-intelligence-ian-goodfellow/. Accessed 7 September 2020

Drahos P (1996a) Global law reform and rent-seeking: the case of intellectual property. Australian Journal of Corporate Law 7(1):45–61

Gabble R, Kohler J C (2014) "To patent or not to patent? " The case of Novartis' cancer drug Glivec in India. Globalization and Health 10(1):3. https://doi.org/10.1186/1744-8603-10-3

Kurzweil R, Jaroch D (1990) The age of intelligent machines. MIT Press, United States

Kusumadara A (2000) Analysis of the Failure of the Implementation of Intellectual Property Laws in Indonesia. Doctor of Philosophy Thesis, University of Sydney. http://hdl.handle.net/2123/820

Lehr D, Ohm P (2017) Playing with the Data: What Legal Scholars Should Learn About Machine Learning. UC Davis Law Review 51:653–717

Lepp A W (1990) Intellectual property rights regimes in Southeast Asia. Journal of Southeast Asia Business 6(11):28–40

Lessig L (2001) The Future of Ideas: The Fate of The Commons in a Connected World. Vintage Books, New York

Levendowski A (2018) How copyright law can fix artificial intelligence's implicit bias problem. Washington Law Review 93:579–630

[58] A smaller scale of production usually involves the creation of generative AI for research purposes at the research centres. While a larger scale of production occurs mostly regarding the creation of generative AI at an industrial level.

Lim D (2018) AI & IP: Innovation & Creativity in an Age of Accelerated Change. Akron Law Review 52:813–875

Lukman J (2019) AI & modest wear: Ria Miranda celebrates 10-year fashion career. The Jakarta Post. https://www.thejakartapost.com/news/2019/11/30/ai-modest-wear-ria-miranda-celebrates-10-year-fashion-career.html. Accessed 4 February 2020

McCutcheon J (2012) The Vanishing Author in Computer-Generated Works: A Critical Analysis of Recent Australian Case Law. Melbourne University Law Review 36:915–969

Minsky M L (1967) Computation: Finite and Infinite Machines. Prentice-Hall, New Jersey

Minsky M L (1986) The Society of Mind. Simon & Schuster, New York

Murphy K P (2012) Machine Learning: A Probabilistic Perspective. MIT Press, Cambridge, Massachusetts

Olewitz C (2019) A Japanese A.I. Program Just Wrote a Short Novel, and It Almost Won a Literary Prize. Digital Trends. https://www.digitaltrends.com/cool-tech/japanese-ai-writes-novel-passes-first-round-nationanl-literary-prize/. Accessed 6 February 2020

Preeg E H (2012) The Uruguay Round Negotiations and the Creation of the WTO. In: Daunton M et al. (eds) The Oxford Handbook on The World Trade Organization. Oxford University Press, Oxford, pp 122–138 https://doi.org/10.1093/oxfordhb/9780199586103.013.0007

Saidin O K (2016) The Choice of Foreign Legal Transplants Policy in Regulating Indonesian Copyright Law: Between Standardization and Coagulation. Mimbar Hukum 27(3):504–516 https://doi.org/10.22146/jmh.15874

Sarahtika D (2019) No More Slaves to Hollywood: Indonesian Films' Upward Trajectory on Global Stage. Jakartaglobe. https://jakartaglobe.id/culture/no-more-slaves-to-hollywood-indonesian-films-upward-trajectory-on-global-stage

Setiawan T S (2015) Ikang Fauzi: Capek-capek Bikin, Malah Dibajak [Ikang Fauzi: Worked Hard to Create Songs, Only for Them to be Pirated]. Kompas. https://entertainment.kompas.com/read/2015/09/22/214153710/Ikang.Fauzi.Capek-capek.Bikin.Malah.Dibajak. Accessed 3 October 2020

Singgih V P (2017) Indonesia expects jump in creative economy by 2019. The Jakarta Post. https://www.thejakartapost.com/news/2017/03/15/indonesia-expects-jump-in-creative-economy-by-2019.html. Accessed 14 April 2021

Singh H et al. (2013) Real-life applications of fuzzy logic. Advances in Fuzzy Systems 2013:1–3. https://doi.org/10.1155/2013/581879

Sobel B L W (2018) Artificial Intelligence's Fair Use Crisis. Columbia Journal of Law & the Arts 41(1):45–97

Statt N (2017) Google is Using AI to Create Stunning Landscape Photos Using Street View Imagery. The Verge. https://www.theverge.com/2017/7/14/15973712/google-ai-research-street-view-panorama-photo-editing. Accessed 16 February 2022

Strategi Nasional Kecerdasan Artifisial, Badan Pengkajian dan Penerapan Teknologi (BPPT) (2020) Strategi Nasional Kecerdasan Artifisial Indonesia Tahun 2020 – 2045 [Indonesia's National Artificial Intelligence Strategy 2020–2045]. BPPT Press, Jakarta

Surden H (2014) Machine Learning and Law. Washington Law Review 89(1):87–115

Turing A M (1950) Computing Machinery and Intelligence. Mind LIX(236):433–460

Chapter 3
Why Protect AI-generated Works?

Contents

Abstract Even though AI-generated works cannot meet copyright's requirement, protecting them remains desirable. This chapter emphasises that the goal of protecting AI-generated works is not to grant rights to non-human entities. Instead, it aims to reward and protect the human contributors behind the generative AI. This argument is justified by both natural and utilitarian approaches, by noting that Indonesian copyright integrates these two approaches in its copyright law. By employing these approaches, the chapter proceeds by analysing who should own AI-generated works: 1) human stakeholders; 2) the generative AI software; or 3) no one. It argues that based on natural and utilitarian theory, human ownership of AI-generated works is more justifiable than software ownership. Further, this chapter also asserts that leaving matters related to AI-generated works to be governed by the public domain would fail to provide incentives and/or protection for their human contributors and, therefore, should not be considered a solution.

Keywords Labour theory · Personality theory · John Locke · Georg Hegel · Karl Marx · Self-alienation · Copyright theory · Legal personhood · Human creativity

3.1 Introduction

While interest in AI-generated works and copyright has recently increased, the academic debate stretches back nearly 40 years.[1] This early software tended to be composed of more simplistic systems that were often limited by rules and reasons

[1] There are six main branches of AI, namely: machine learning, neural networks, robotics, expert systems, fuzzy logic, and natural language processing (Tyagi 2020).

L. Andrini, *Protecting Artificial Intelligence-generated Works in Indonesia*, Information Technology and Law Series 41, https://doi.org/10.1007/978-94-6265-703-8_3

programmed into the code. Additionally, the number of developers involved in the creation of the systems were more limited and users often had higher levels of technological skill sets. As such, these factors made it easier to trace how a particular result was achieved or an object produced.[2] This had consequences for assigning copyright as it was easier to determine the party who had most contributed to the end result. In contrast, this project looks at the question of copyright in AI-generated works as it occurs within Indonesia. One of the consequences of how generative AI software operates is that the impact of the 'machine's logic' needs to be distinguished from the role that human intervention plays in producing AI-generated works. This, in turn, may influence whether that work is 1) protected by copyright and 2) if so, who should be nominated as the author of the work.

This book finds that AI-generated works need protection for three main reasons. First, despite the myth that such works are created autonomously without any human intervention or contribution, the process actually involves multiple parties.[3] These parties often invest a considerable amount of time and money in creating AI-generated works and as a consequence want to be compensated by proprietary rights. Second, an ownership right for users of generative AI is necessary to protect their investment in making AI-generated works. Third, AI-generated works have the potential to be misused by their creators or a third party, for example to create a deepfake or spread misinformation. A proprietary interest would allow the public or the state to readily identify a creator-owner who is misusing an AI-generated work and assign responsibility. It would allow an owner whose work is misused by a third party to pursue damages against that party.[4]

Copyright's requirements of authorship and creativity are central issues in the attempt to protect AI-generated works. This is because although the creation of AI-generated works often involves many people occupying different roles, the results of their labour is not necessarily visible in the outcome. Accordingly, some argue that AI-generated works should be deemed an independent creation of a software programme requiring a minimal human contribution. This troubles the creativity requirement of Indonesian copyright, an attribute long presumed to be an aspect of only human ingenuity. In addressing these challenges, the distinctive features of Indonesia's law are considered, such as its 1) historical, and economic and socio-cultural backgrounds; 2) national ideology; as well as its 3) national objectives to foster people's welfare.

Furthermore, as the law realistically needs to respond to AI-generated works as a new object of protection, the law needs to consider the different views of software developers, data trainers, and users of generative AI.[5] While it might not be possible

---

[2] See Farr 1989; Miller 1993; Wu 1997.

[3] Fraser 2016.

[4] Throughout 2023, there were some deepfake images affecting public confidence, for example the image of Donald Trump being arrested or the explosion at the Pentagon, see Stanley-Becker and Nix 2023; Bond 2023.

[5] Indonesia's early development of copyright law has shown that when the law did not reflect people's interests and socio-technical realities, it would hardly be enforceable.

to accommodate all interests, the law should at least reflect most stakeholders' views so that what it implements and thus enforces is better supported.[6] To better understand their views, the fieldwork of this research consisting of the interviewing of generative AI developers, data trainers, users and representatives from relevant Indonesian institutions related to intellectual property and technological development to better understand their views. The findings from this fieldwork were analysed to understand whether the stakeholders' interests are reflected in the current copyright law and, if not, how the law might be changed to accommodate their understandings of the AI-generated works' creation process.

At the international level, there is substantial, if not universal, agreement that copyright protections apply to creative works that are fixed, original, and a result of intellectual/creative efforts.[7] The term 'fixation' is understood as an act that finalises the work in a tangible medium or expression that allows for it to be reproduced or distributed.[8] 'Originality' means that the author independently created the work and, in doing so, did not copy from other existing works.[9] Although not explicitly stated, these requirements imply that copyright protects works that are produced by human authors. Thus, they may challenge the assessing of copyright protection of AI-generated works as their production renders human involvement in, and contribution to, the creative process unclear. As a result, numerous issues arise about whether AI-generated works can or should attract copyright protections. These issues include who should be granted controlling interests, whether that stakeholder or another group should be considered an 'author', and whether the data used to train the generative AI should also receive some sort of protection.

3.2 Philosophical Justifications of Intellectual Property Rights and Copyright

The popular conception is that the primary legal function of intellectual property is to protect the intangible products of mental labour.[10] This purpose is legally accomplished through numerous mechanisms that are grouped under the single category of intellectual property. Significantly, each of proprietary mechanism has distinct

[6] In general, it is argued that society's acceptance plays an important part in the enforcement of copyright law, for without such acceptance, they would not feel morally bound to the law and this might result in the non-conformity to the law, see Ouma 2006. In the context of Indonesia, history has shown that when the copyright law did not reflect people's interests, it was hardly implementable and resulted in massive copyright infringements, as for instance during the 1980s, see Kusumadara 2000.

[7] Goldstein and Hugenholtz 2010, p. 4.

[8] Brown 2018, p. 17.

[9] In some jurisdictions, such as the United States, originality also requires a certain degree of creativity put into the work, see ibid.

[10] Bently and Sherman 2014, pp. 4–36.

requirements, is animated according to a logic, and confers different rights. Copyright is the intellectual property mechanism that specifically protects literary and artistic property resulting from the mental labour.[11] Although termed *property*, intellectual property stands as a distinct type of proprietary interest whose features overlap with, but are also differentiated from, those of real or tangible property in primary ways. This distinction has triggered numerous scholarly debates comparing the legal issues of real to intellectual property. Research finding against attributing property being produced through mental labour holds that intellectual property might not be a property *per se* because it lacks physical form, and can neither be acquired by an occupation often performed upon real property.[12] Yet, more recent research attempts to justify intellectual property because the labour associated with the work generates proprietary rights.[13] In supporting this, two main theories are often used to justify intellectual property philosophically. On the one hand, 'labour theory', is a powerful philosophical framework for contemporary intellectual property law in most Anglo-Saxon jurisprudence.[14] On the other, 'personality theory', which is deeply rooted in continental jurisprudence, including Dutch law, influenced Indonesia's modern legal system.[15]

Labour theory, often linked to John Locke, asserts that property rights result from combining a person's labour with a natural object.[16] Locke is interpreted in two ways most often used to explain and justify intellectual property law: first, that the unpleasantness of labour *should* be rewarded with property.[17] On the other hand, the instrumental interpretation of labour theory asserts that the unpleasantness of labour should be rewarded to motivate people to perform labour.[18] Although the two approaches may seem different, they can co-exist in that the normative interpretation grants property rights for works that have already been performed, while the instrumental interpretation grants property rights to encourage the performance of future works.

In contrast to Locke, Georg Hegel's personality theory justifies intellectual property on the basis that property is an expression of the self.[19] Hegel believes that the mind and its abilities are internal to a person. Further, expressions of a person's mental ability can result in something external and, in this way, be alienated from the creator.[20] Regarding copyright, Hegelian alienation is manifested in two ways:

---

[11] Ibid.

[12] Sherman and Bently 1999, pp. 20–24.

[13] Ibid.

[14] Hughes 1988, p. 288.

[15] Ibid.

[16] Rose 1985, pp. 73–74.

[17] Hughes 1988.

[18] Ibid.

[19] Ibid. p. 288.

[20] The alienation of property also exists in Karl Marx's idea of property that a private property is an outcome of externalised, alienated labour (Drahos 1996b).

the first is to alienate all rights to property through sale.[21] The second is to alienate the copies of property with restrictions, such as selling copies of copyrighted book for personal use by the purchaser.[22]

While Hegel views alienation as a process of self-discovery, Karl Marx views this concept as corrupting an individual's nature as a labourer,[23] in that such alienation separates labour from the self of the labourer.[24] He further asserts that, in producing commodities, the labourer turns themself into a commodity:

> '[...] the *increasing value* of the world of things proceeds in direct proportion (to) the *devaluation* of the world of men. Labour produces not only commodities; it produces itself and the worker as *commodity* – and does so in the proportion in which it produces commodities generally.'[25]

The concept of alienation makes it possible for someone to privately own things produced by the labour of others, which Marx ultimately viewed as problematic and the source of class tension in the capitalist system.[26] Thus, Marxian scholars of intellectual property argue that the alienation of an individual's intellectual labour, like physical labour, is problematic. Yet the notion of alienated labour is common in intellectual property, such as in copyright being made-for-hire. Under this situation, an employee transfers copyright interests in any work created during employment to their employer. In light of Marx's theory of alienation, employer's ownership of the works created by his/her employee alienates the employees from their own intellectual labour. The employees who trade the labour of their intellectual ability in exchange of money are treated as a commodity and are thus prone to be exploited.

While intellectual property is similar to real property, there are some instances where the former operates according to a different logic.[27] This is true for copyright, a type of intellectual property that is often justified by two main principles, namely, natural rights and utilitarian principle. Civil law countries, such as the Netherlands, Germany and Indonesia, tend to rely on the principle of natural rights, while common law countries such as the United States, the United Kingdom and Australia base their copyright law on utilitarian principles.[28] From the perspective of natural rights, an author is central to the creation of the work so that his/her personality is assumed to be reflected in the work.[29] This results in the author being strongly connected to the work that is honoured through copyright, in particular according to moral rights.[30]

---

[21] Hughes 1988.

[22] Ibid.

[23] Radin 1982, p. 982.

[24] Radin 1987, pp. 1871–1872.

[25] Ibid.

[26] Radin 1982, p. 981.

[27] In the realm of copyright law, for example, a person may have property rights over the music CDs he/she bought; still, they are prohibited from ripping the songs in the CDs simply because he/she does not have copyright rights over them.

[28] Goldstein and Hugenholtz 2010.

[29] Senftleben 2018, p. 415.

[30] Ibid.

From a natural rights perspective, as moral rights are integral to the author, they remain with the author even though the economic rights are transferred to another party. Moral rights grant the author rights to be acknowledged as the creator of the work, to retain its contents, and to alter his/her work. On the other hand, common law countries prioritise the utilitarian purpose of copyright that purport to more greatly benefit society.[31] To serve this purpose, copyright is granted to promote the creation and public accessibility of works.

Despite these differences, Martin Senftleben argues that while any one of these theories might dominate in a particular jurisdiction, most national copyright laws actually reflect a mixture of both natural law and utilitarian approaches.[32] Some common law countries that tend to prioritise utilitarian logic also accommodate some natural rights in their legislation. Similarly, some civil law countries may also have adopted a utilitarian purpose in their legislations. In her essay, *Tales of Two Copyright*, Jane Ginsburg elaborates how the formation of US copyright law focused on both public and private rights. She located her argument in a *Document Illustrative of the Formation of the Union* dated 18 August 1787 that states "the proposed legislative powers were submitted to the Committee of Detail to secure literary authors their copy rights for a limited time, to encourage by proper premiums and provisions the advancement of useful knowledge and discoveries."[33] According to Ginsburg, this shows an intention to balance the protection of the authors' rights, for their labour within the work, and for the public's access to knowledge. In contrast, some civil law countries, including Indonesia, have adopted the idea that copyright is a means to foster intellectual progress.[34]

The approach adopted by a legal system has consequences. Specifically, Ginsburg argues that the natural rights approach is more author-oriented and, thus leads to a stronger copyright system with more robust protection in the sense that a higher threshold of authorial contribution may be required.[35] An author-oriented copyright system usually sets more subjective requirements for a work to be protected, such as the author's personality being connected to the work he/she creates. In contrast, copyright systems that adopt the utilitarian foundation focus more on protecting works and less on subjective requirements to establish copyright protection. This approach is more socially-oriented, thus capable of protecting a wider variety of works, some of which might be deemed to have lower levels of authorial contribution (e.g., compilations).[36]

Indonesian copyright law combines both natural rights and utilitarian principles. On the one hand, the law requires that works reflect the author's personality while, on the other, Indonesian law also views copyright as a means to foster social and cultural

[31] Ibid.

[32] Ibid.

[33] 1 Documents Illustrative of the Formation of the Union, *H.R. Doc. No. 398, 69th Congress, 1st Session. 130 (1927)* in Ginsburg 1989.

[34] Senftleben 2018.

[35] Ginsburg 1989.

[36] Ibid.

welfare. In this sense, Indonesian copyright law seeks to uphold and balance private rights and contribute to a broader interest. Articulating and striking this balance regarding the underlying principles of copyright significantly challenges determining how the law should respond to and accommodate a new object of protection, such as AI-generated works.[37]

3.3 Copyright and Technological Change: Application to Computer-generated Works

As discussed earlier, technological change often challenges long-held social norms, by altering common-sense presumptions and, in some cases, prompting legal change. A classic example of this relationship between technological, social, and legal change discussed by Lawrence Lessig pertains to the invention of flight. Before it was invented, common law doctrine pertaining to land ownership was understood to attribute the proprietor with absolute control over not only the surface of his property, but also nearly complete dominion over the subsurface below and above air.[38] Yet, subsequent to commercial flight, Justice William Douglas of the United States Supreme Court in *United States v Causby* (1946) found that the common law principle of infinite ownership above and below ground "had no place in the modern world." Instead, ownership required boundaries otherwise "common sense [would] revolt at the idea" since such a definition would interfere with the public interest in air travel and expose any flight operator to an unreasonable number of suits.[39] Lessig uses this example to argue that the widely and long-held doctrine may be irrelevant when faced with a new socio-technical phenomenon, thus necessitating legal change.

Throughout the 20th and into the 21st century, technological change has repeatedly challenged copyright. The development of novel forms of recording technology, for example, has impacted upon the manner in which a producer or copyright holder can circulate protected content to an audience. In some cases, this development removed the distinction between these parties to the extent that audiences not only consume content, but are also able to produce it as well. In this sense, the neat divide between consumer and producer presents distinctive challenges to the underlying reasons and practical operation of copyright law. As Bernt Hugenholtz noted, while historically copyright aimed to regulate commercial actors, this was challenged by technological

---

[37] In particular on how an AI-generated work may be seen as an extension of its author's personality and at the same time be used to support national development.

[38] This change is recorded in the Causbys case where North Carolina farmers, Thomas Lee and Tinie Causby, filed a lawsuit on the grounds that the government had trespassed on their land. This lawsuit was based on the concept that land ownership extended beyond the surface of the land, so included the air above it. So, when military aircraft flew over the Causbys' farm, causing stress and death of the chicken, the Causbys felt that the government had trespassed on their private property, see Lessig 2004.

[39] Lessig 2004.

developments such as the tape-to-tape player which required the law to take account of the interests of consumers as well.[40]

Similar challenges are presented by the advance in AI, through its generative ability that allows a user (i.e., the putative *consumer* of the software) to *produce* a novel work (e.g., a song), simply by executing the program.[41] While this might be similar to previous technologies (e.g., phonogram recorders) which collapsed the boundary between consumers and producers, the operation of generative AI differs in two important respects. First, it requires even less direct user involvement to produce AI-generated works: all that is required is that the user simply follow the prompting of the program. Second, to be able to produce new outcomes, requires large amounts of training data to be sorted and classified, a labour-intensive process that in some cases requires significant skill and/or judgment.[42] Moreover, training data sets must be curated by data scientists,[43] a role that relates generally to AI-generated works and specifically to the roles played by generative AI's programmers and users.[44] The presence of data trainers, adds more complexity to the analysis of copyright protection as it not only introduces a third role to AI-generated works' creation, but also increases the likelihood of multiple authorial contributions to the final output because they may include numerous people. In some cases, the training data might notably entail proprietary or copyright protection that can potentially be reflected in AI-generated works.[45]

Contemporarily, an author is almost always presumed to be the owner of a copyright protected work unless he/she decides to transfer his/her rights and convey them to another party. This presumption is challenged by the existence of AI-generated works, where authorship is unclear: *is the work authored by software? one of the humans working behind or with the software?* or *some other parties?* Any of these options can potentially ignite further debate. If the software is considered the 'author' of the AI-generated works, issues arise concerning whether software might attract legal personhood. On the other hand, if humans are treated as authors of the work, determining who might qualify as the rightful author(s) of the AI-generated works is challenging. Even if an author of an AI-generated work is identifiable, a secondary challenge remains as to whether that party should be treated as an owner in the typical sense or whether specialised rights might accrue under copyright law.

---

[40] Hugenholtz 2012.

[41] This is only an extreme example where consumers only perform none to minimum efforts in the creation of the work. However, there are also AI-systems that require consumers to determine parameters which will be reflected in the end result of the work.

[42] Lehr and Ohm 2017, p. 677.

[43] Ibid.

[44] It is possible for the same individual to occupy all three roles, namely programmer, data trainer, and software user, involved in the use of ML software to produce AI-generated works. However, it is important to note that these are all distinct roles and that as the complexity of the software increases, so does the likelihood that different, and potentially numerous, individuals occupy each of these roles.

[45] Samuelson 1986.

In recent years, there has been growing interest in the application of copyright law to AI-generated works. Despite this, there has not been a unified response from either scholars or policy makers about how such issues might be resolved has occurred. In general, the responses can be classified into the following three categories: 1) one of the humans involved in the generation of AI-generated works should be recognised as the copyright owner; 2) the generative AI used to create the works should be recognised as the copyright owner; and 3) there should be no copyright protection for AI-generated works.

a) *A human stakeholder as the copyright owner*

One argument is that the copyright of AI-generated works should be assigned to the human authors involved in the process.[46] Andrew Ventimiglia proposes an *a posteriori* model of authorship. Instead of using the traditional copyright approach that presumes authors are the source of a work, Ventimiglia's model firstly acknowledges the emergence of the work as a legal-material object, before legally analysing to find the legal author of the work.[47] Regarding AI-generated works, this approach to determine authorial status focuses on the programmers or the software user involved in creating the work and assigning copyright to one of these two roles.

Under this argument, programmers of generative AI make the most important contribution to the generated works and therefore should be entitled to copyright protection.[48] According to this logic, programmers are the most significant contributors because they set the conditions that allow generative AI to operate and generate work. Specifically, programmers initially set generative AI's objectives, create the algorithm and turn it into the user-friendly software necessary for it to function.[49] In justifying the programmers' copyright over AI-generated works, some scholars look to the works made-for-hire policy,[50] commonly used

---

[46] Two of the proponents of such an idea are Jane Ginsburg and Ali Budiardjo, who argued that questioning the possibility of machine authorship may cause confusion in the discussions on copyright and AI-generated works. Instead, the discussion proposed was to look for the human author in AI-generated works, see Ginsburg and Budiardjo 2019.

[47] This was modelled after the infamous *Urantia v. Maaherra* case, a case concerning the dispute over *The Urantia Book*, which was believed to have been written by celestial authors through the medium of human beings. The celestial authors inspired multiple anonymous (human) authors, called the Conduit, to write on their behalf. Thirty years later, these works were compiled into *The Urantia Book* and published by a group called Contact Commission. The Commission filed a lawsuit against Kirsten Maaherra after she had distributed the infringing copies of the book on compact disks, assuming that the book was not subject to copyright because it was written by non-human authors. However, the court decided that *The Urantia Book* was copyrightable as the involvement of Contact Commission fulfils the minimum threshold of creativity as required by copyright (Ventimiglia 2020).

[48] Yu 2017

[49] Ibid.

[50] The use of the work-made-for-hire doctrine to justify the programmers' copyright is based on the logic that the AI-generated works are not directly generated by the programmer. Due to such indirect authorship, there needs to be a justification to extend the programmers' rights over AI-generated works, thus the work-made-for-hire doctrine is used (Huson 2018).

in the United States. This considers the employer to be the legal author of a work despite not being the author-in-fact.[51] In other words, the programmers are analogous to the employers, while the generative AI is analogous to the employee.[52] Accordingly, the copyright of AI works generated by the software belong to the programmers. However, the main challenge in applying a work made-for-hire policy is establishing an employment relationship between programmers and software as both parties do not enjoy and perform the rights and obligations similar to an employer–employee relationship.[53]

Alternatively, programmers' copyright can be justified by the argument that copyright should be granted to those who have made the arrangements necessary to produce AI-generated works.[54] This argument has been adopted in British copyright law which provides that 'in the case of a literary, dramatic, musical, or artistic works which is computer-generated, the author shall be taken to be the person whose arrangements necessary for creating the work are undertaken.'[55] However, in the context of AI-generated works, which involve multiple people with different roles, it is unclear who makes the necessary arrangements and, as such, should be rewarded with copyright ownership. On the one hand, programmers who have designed and trained the program may be deemed as having 'arrangement necessary' to creating AI-generated works, even though they do not directly contribute to creating AI-generated works.[56]

In some situations, the software users' role may also need to be considered when assessing copyright in an AI-generated works. Specifically, in some circumstances, a user may do more than *merely* execute the software[57] and this effort may entitle them to copyright in the resulting AI-generated works. Historically, technology users have been considered authors of a work and are thus deemed to merit a copyright interest. The underlying reason is that the users

[51] Grimmelmann 2016, p. 400.

[52] Ibid.

[53] The complexities of establishing an employment relationship between the programmers and the ML/AI software are highlighted by Huson who asserts that the programmers, as employees, do not need to give employment benefits to the software. Moreover, the absence of agreement between the programmers and the software related to working hours, the duration of the contract, remuneration, and so on, may hamper the application of the work-made-for-hire doctrine into a programmers-software relationship (Huson 2018, p. 73).

[54] The basic idea of this argument has been adopted into national law by countries such as the United Kingdom, New Zealand, India, Hong Kong, and Ireland (White and Matulionyte 2020).

[55] *S 9(3), Copyright, Designs, and Patents Act 1988* (*United Kingdom*) (Copyright, Designs, and Patents Act).

[56] Lehr and Ohm classified the generation of works using machine-learning algorithms into two main workflows, namely 'playing with the data' and the 'running model'. 'Playing with the data' covers the initial stage of determining the software's main function, the coding, the gathering of relevant data to train the software, as well as the training process. Meanwhile the 'running model' is the stage where the software is ready to be deployed and to generate its own decisions/works (Lehr and Ohm 2017).

[57] This is often referred to as 'pressing the button'.

have employed the technology[58] and fixed the work in a tangible medium.[59] A prime example of this is a photographer who holds copyright over photographs that they have captured.[60] Another example might be a videographer who merely presses a button to record a performance but is considered the author of that recording.[61]

AI-generated works present a further complication compared to photographs and videos in that such works often involve numerous parties with different inputs and competing interests. In relation to photographs, the question around copyright is socially and legally straightforward and well-settled; namely, the photographer becomes an author through their control of the camera that produces the result: irrespective of the effort they put into its framing, lighting or other resources.[62] In contrast, producing AI-generated works involves different parties that perform different roles in developing the work. Because different parties may contribute differently to the final work, they may have competing interests in the resulting copyright work.

A final challenge for assigning copyright in AI-generated works pertains to the situation whereby generative AI has significantly more autonomy than earlier forms of technology, such as the camera or tape-recorder. As a result, generative AI may be capable of producing its own decisions and shaping the resulting work despite being controlled by the user.[63] This autonomy destabilises the users' position as author of the AI-generated works.

b) *Software as the copyright owner*

The second argument suggests that generative AI might be assigned the status of author of the work it generates and thus be the owner of the resulting copyright. This is based on the idea that the software connects directly to the resulting AI-generated works since it is important to its fixation.[64] In contrast, programmers and users merely develop and then execute the program in the initial stage of AI-generated works' creation. This argument triggers further legal questions: *Why would generative AI be given copyright? Should it be given legal personhood?*[65]

---

[58] Miller 1993.

[59] Samuelson 1986, p. 1202.

[60] Miller 1993.

[61] Samuelson 1986.

[62] The question is less complex when compared to the challenges brought by AI-generated works in the sense that there are only two possibilities in answering such a question: 1) the photographer is the author of the photograph so he is entitled to be protected by copyright; or 2) the photographer is not the author because the photograph is made by a machine and therefore it should go directly to the public domain. In *Burrow-Giles Lithographic Co. v. Sarony*, for example, Sarony's position as an author of the photograph of Oscar Wilde was questioned. It was argued that the photograph was produced by a machine and not supposed to be protected by copyright. The judge in Supreme Court finally decided so (Samuelson 1986).

[63] Yu argued that the users do not make a real decision when using ML/AI software to generate AI-generated works (Yu 2017).

[64] Ibid; Wu 1997.

[65] A relevant example on how non-legal persons did not enjoy intellectual property rights over their creation may be traced back to the 18th century during the enslavement period in Northern

If so, can its work fulfil the originality and creativity requirement as set by copyright law? One justification of copyright law is to encourage the production of new works, an argument that presumes a human author requires a proprietary interest as an incentive to create.[66] This incentive cannot be applied to generative AI as software only produces new works when users execute the program.[67] As generative AI does not need to be incentivised or compensated, this argument renders copyright protection redundant.

Another problem in attributing copyright to software is that it requires the law to acknowledge software as a legal subject and thus sets boundaries on the software's rights and obligations. This includes problems in granting personality to the software,[68] determining its responsibility and ability to appear before the court,[69] and the duration of copyright protection for non-human subjects.[70] Software's legal personhood challenges the attribution of copyright to software because, so far, copyright has only been rewarded to authors having legal personalities.[71] In responding to such a challenge, Shlomit Yanisky-Ravid proposes that legal reform recognise generative AI's copyright over its creations.[72] Similarly, Robert Yu argues that granting authorship to generative AI may be consistent with the notion of granting copyright to parties who have contributed their intellectual and creative efforts to works.[73] However, radical change would be required to the contemporary copyright regime because it both presents a new authorial entity and may produce legal uncertainty. One of the required changes relates to the originality requirement set by copyright,[74] which is closely linked to human ability and the assumption that creative works emanate from an author's mind, not copied from someone else's works.[75] Furthermore, a higher threshold of originality, which some research supports, would require the author to have

America. At that time, slaves were seen as property, thus they did not possess legal personhood. The Confederate Patent Act granted patent rights for the inventions of African-American slaves to the owner of the slave (Reddix-Smalls 2018).

[66] Samuelson 1986.

[67] Schönberger 2018.

[68] Davies 2011.

[69] Hristov 2017, p. 441.

[70] Huson 2018.

[71] For example, in *Naruto v. Slater*, the Court refused copyright protection of photographs taken by a monkey because of its lack of legal personhood (*Naruto v. Slater, 888 F.3d 418*).

[72] Yanisky-Ravid argued that so far 'the current legal regime focuses only on what was relevant in the past, namely the human authors behind the creative process. When this traditional approach has been implemented for assessing robots' creations, policymakers have considered the human behind the creative robot's works and declared that person to be the creator and therefore entitled to copyright protection.' In Yanisky-Ravid and Velez-Hernandez 2018.

[73] Yu 2017, pp. 1257–1258.

[74] Butler 1982, p. 719.

[75] Ginsburg 2003.

the 'intention to create the work'.[76] This means that such intentionality would arguably be absent in the operation of generative AI.

c) *Nobody holds copyright over AI-generated works and the work goes straight to the public domain*
The third argument is to refuse copyright protection to AI-generated works and to automatically place this type of work in the public domain once generated. The justification for this argument is that such works are made by non-human subjects, while copyright honours humans as authors of creative works.[77] Proponents of this line of argument suggest that AI-generated works would provide a public benefit by contributing to the public domain and, as such, would help to advance human creativity.[78] However, this also comes with disadvantages as people who work behind the AI-generated works might not be fairly compensated for their labours.[79] Additionally, some argue that the programmers have already obtained copyright from the generative AI's code, that is the mechanism through which an AI-generated work is created. According to this argument, the programmers are already incentivised and compensated through software copyright.[80] However, creating AI-generated works does not only involve the programmers, because the users and/or the data trainers may also contribute their labour and, as a result, have economic interests in the resulting AI-generated works. In this sense, leaving AI-generated works to the public domain might jeopardise the interests of the parties who work behind the software.

References

Bently L, Sherman B (2014) Intellectual Property Law, 4th edn. Oxford University Press

Bond S (2023) Fake viral images of an explosion at the Pentagon were probably created by AI. National Public Radio. https://www.npr.org/2023/05/22/1177590231/fake-viral-images-of-an-explosion-at-the-pentagon-were-probably-created-by-ai. Accessed 29 July 2023

Brown N I (2018) Artificial Authors: A Case for Copyright in Computer-Generated Works. The Columbia Science and Technology Law Review 20:1–41 https://doi.org/10.7916/stlr.v20i1.4766

Butler T L (1982) Can a Computer be an Author? Copyright Aspects of Artificial Intelligence. Hastings Communications and Entertainment Law Journal 4(4):707–747

Davies C R (2011) An evolutionary step in intellectual property rights – Artificial intelligence and intellectual property. Computer Law & Security Review 27(6):601–619 https://doi.org/10.1016/j.clsr.2011.09.006

Drahos P (1996b) A philosophy of intellectual property. ANU eText, Acton 2601

[76] Yanisky-Ravid and Velez-Hernandez 2018.

[77] Huson 2018.

[78] Ibid., p. 77.

[79] Daryl Lim points out that when AI-generated works fall into the public domain, it could 'devastate the incentives to invest in AI-generated works.' In Lim 2018.

[80] Those who are supportive of this argument think that attributing copyright to the programmers may create a problem of over-rewarding the programmers and, at the same time, prevent society from enjoying the work (Davies 2011).

Farr E H (1989) Copyrightability of computer-created works. Rutgers Computer & Technology Law Journal 15(1):63–80
Fraser E (2016) Computers as Inventors – Legal and Policy Implications of Artificial Intelligence on Patent Law. SCRIPTed 13(3):305–333 https://doi.org/10.2966/scrip.130316.305
Ginsburg J C (1989) Tale of Two Copyrights: Literary Property in Revolutionary France and America. Tulane Law Review 64(5):991–1031
Ginsburg J C (2003) The Concept of Authorship in Comparative Copyright Law. DePaul Law Review 52(4):1063–1092
Ginsburg J C, Budiardjo L A (2019) Authors and Machines. Berkeley Technology Law Journal 34(2):343–448
Goldstein P, Hugenholtz P B (2010) International copyright: Principles, Law and Practice, 2nd edn. Oxford University Press, Oxford
Grimmelmann J (2016) There's No Such Thing as a Computer-Authored Work - And It's a Good Thing, Too. Columbia Journal of Law & Arts 39(3):403–416
Hugenholtz P B (2012) The Story of The Tape Recorder and The History of Copyright Levies. In: Sherman B, Wiseman L (eds) Copyright and the Challenge of the New. Kluwer Law International, The Netherlands, pp 179–196
Hughes J (1988) The Philosophy of Intellectual Property. Georgetown Law Journal 77(2):287
Hristov K (2017) Artificial intelligence and the copyright dilemma. IDEA: The IP Law Review 57(3):431–454
Huson G (2018) I, Copyright. Santa Clara High Technology Law Journal 35(2):54–78
Kusumadara A (2000) Analysis of the Failure of the Implementation of Intellectual Property Laws in Indonesia. Doctor of Philosophy Thesis, University of Sydney. http://hdl.handle.net/2123/820
Lehr D, Ohm P (2017) Playing with the Data: What Legal Scholars Should Learn About Machine Learning. UC Davis Law Review 51:653–717
Lessig L (2004) Free Culture: How Big Media Uses Technology and the Law to Lock Down Culture and Control Creativity. Penguin Press
Lim D (2018) AI & IP: Innovation & Creativity in an Age of Accelerated Change. Akron Law Review 52:813–875
Miller A R (1993) Copyright Protection for Computer Programs, Databases, and Computer-Generated Works: Is Anything New Since CONTU?. Harvard Law Review 106(5):977–1073 https://doi.org/10.2307/1341682
Ouma M N (2006) Optimal Enforcement of Music Copyright in Sub-Saharan Africa: Reality or a Myth? The Journal of World Intellectual Property 9(5):592–627 https://doi.org/10.1111/j.1422-2213.2006.00304.x
Radin M J (1982) Property and Personhood. Stanford Law Review 34(5):957–1015 https://doi.org/10.2307/1228541
Radin M J (1987) Market-inalienability. Harvard Law Review 100(8):1849–1937 https://doi.org/10.2307/1341192
Reddix-Smalls B (2018) Intellectual Property, Income Inequality, and Societal Interconnectivity in the United States: Social Calculus and the Historical Distribution of Wealth. North Carolina Central University Science & Intellectual Property Law Review 11(1):1–48
Rose M (1985) Possession as the Origin of Property. The University of Chicago Law Review 52(1):73–88 https://doi.org/10.2307/1599571
Samuelson P (1986) Allocating Ownership Rights in Computer-Generated Works. University of Pittsburgh Law Review 47:1185–1228
Schönberger D (2018) Deep Copyright: Up- and Downstream Questions Related to Artificial Intelligence (AI) and Machine Learning (ML). Droit d'auteur 4.04 / Copyright 4.0 145–173
Senftleben M (2018) More Money for Creators and More Support for Copyright in Society-Fair Remuneration Rights in Germany and the Netherlands. Columbia Journal of Law & Arts 41(3):413–433
Sherman B, Bently L (1999) The Making of Modern Intellectual Property Law: The British Experience, 1760–1911. Cambridge University Press, Cambridge, UK

Stanley-Becker I, Nix N (2023) Fake images of Trump arrest show 'giant step' for AI's disruptive power. The Washington Post. https://www.washingtonpost.com/politics/2023/03/22/trump-arrest-deepfakes/. Accessed 10 October 2023

Tyagi N (2020) 6 Major Branches of Artificial Intelligence (AI). Analytic Steps. https://www.analyticssteps.com/blogs/6-major-branches-artificial-intelligence-ai. Accessed 13 January 2021

Ventimiglia A (2020) The Angel in the Machine: Divining Legal Authorship in Channelled and Computer-Generated Works. In: Voss E (ed) Mediality on Trial: Testing and Contesting Trance and Other Media Techniques. De Gruyter Oldenbourg, Berlin/Boston, pp 236–260 https://doi.org/10.1515/9783110416411-009

White C, Matulionyte R (2020) Artificial Intelligence Painting The Bigger Picture For Copyright Ownership. Australian Intellectual Property Journal 30:181–247

Wu A J (1997) From Video Games to Artificial Intelligence: Assigning Copyright Ownership to Works Generated by Increasingly Sophisticated Computer Programs. AIPLA Quarterly Journal 25(1):131–178

Yanisky-Ravid S, Velez-Hernandez L A (2018) Copyrightability of Artworks Produced by Creative Robots and Originality: The Formality-Objective Model. Minnesota Journal of Law, Science and Technology 19(1):1–53

Yu R (2017) The machine author: what level of copyright protection is appropriate for fully independent computer-generated works? University of Pennsylvania Law Review 165(5):1245–1270

Chapter 4
Moral and Economic Rights in Artificial Intelligence-generated Works

Contents

Abstract Economic and moral rights are inherent to copyright law, both in Indonesia and in the EU. Economic rights protect the financial interests of the copyright owner, while moral rights safeguard the authors' attribution and integrity of their works. This chapter contends that while economic rights can be assigned to the human contributors behind AI-generated works, moral rights cannot. Economic rights of AI-generated works are best attributed to the users of generative AI for two reasons. First, economic rights compensate users for their efforts in creating AI-generated works. Second, these rights incentivise users to produce more works, thereby increasing the demand for generative AI in the long run. Meanwhile, moral rights originate from the notion of romantic authorship, which asserts an inseparable connection between an author and their work. The inseparable connection presents a challenge in establishing the necessary connection between the creator and the AI-generated works to justify the attribution of moral rights. The discussion in this chapter proceeds by investigating the potential for recognising users of generative AI as holders of moral rights, but concludes that it might not be possible, given that users may not directly produce the works. Furthermore, attributing moral rights to generative AI software is not feasible, as the software lacks the personality that can be reflected in the work.

Keywords Moral rights · Economic rights · Copyright · Indonesian copyright law · EU copyright · Attribution · Generative AI · Originality · Authorship · Creativity

L. Andrini, *Protecting Artificial Intelligence-generated Works in Indonesia*, Information Technology and Law Series 41, https://doi.org/10.1007/978-94-6265-703-8_4

4.1 Introduction

On 24 October 2019, a Jakarta-based fashion designer, used a generative AI system, named *Rinna,* to produce a new range of scarfs in celebrating a particular milestone in her career.[1] According to the designer, who is well-known in Indonesia for producing ready-to-wear hijabs, she viewed this engagement with generative AI as a collaboration between humans and technology through which she created her artistic product. In this collaboration, the designer engaged with the generative AI system to produce the scarf patterns after which the designer selected, edited, and printed the patterns onto a fabric that he/she selected.[2] This collaboration challenges the myth that generative AI systems are capable of operating in a fully autonomous manner and do not require direct human intervention or engagement in creating AI-generated works. In many cases, human participation is necessary to direct the software and to select from varied outputs. This participation and engagement with the generative AI software can add significant economic value to the AI-generated works. In the case described above, involving the designer-*Rinna* collaboration, the scarf patterns would not have been able to attract economic value, unless selected, printed on a textile, and sold to the public. In the vast majority of cases involving AI-generated works, a human author's efforts will be necessary to ensure that the work is circulated amongst the public in such a way that it is capable of generating economic value. Additionally, having a human author collaborating with generative AI would also mean that he or she would be able to maintain his/her moral rights - including the right to be acknowledged as the author of the works and the right to ensure that the integrity of the work is maintained.

This chapter focuses on the challenges that generative AI and AI-generated works pose to the economic and moral rights in copyright law. It also identifies which stakeholders, if any, have a significant enough input, both in terms of quantity and quality, into the creation of AI-generated works such that they are deserving some form of economic and/or moral interest. In assessing economic rights, I draw from John Locke's labour theory and policy-oriented approaches that copyright, as a fictional monopoly, encourages creative activity. These perspectives provide a framework to determine the parties that should be compensated for their labour and incentivised to produce more works in the future. Using this theoretical framework, this book proposes that generative AI users are the most-qualified stakeholder for being awarded economic rights because they have contributed both their skill and monetary capacity in creating AI-generated works. In terms of determining attribution of moral rights, my analysis focuses on the inseparable connection between author and his/her work to assess. Using this framework, I suggest that generative AI software and the AI-generated works may be inseparably connected. However, this argument is problematic under current Indonesian copyright law and deserves further assessment since generative AI does not qualify for legal personhood. As such, generative AI

[1] Lukman 2019.

[2] Ibid.

software would not be eligible to obtain and hold moral rights in the resulting AI-generated works. Instead, it might be that other stakeholders involved in the creation of the generative AI software could receive these moral rights. However, identifying these other stakeholders would need to proceed on a case-by-case basis given the variation and number of individuals involved in the creation, training, and deployment of generative AI.

As a result, the third section of this chapter explores the possibility for recognizing multiple authors in relation to AI-generated works. To do this, I discuss how the Indonesian Copyright Act addresses works involving multiple authors via its definition of 'author' and note there are numerous Indonesian Copyright Register regularly records multiple authors for a single work. Based upon these parameters, this book finds it is possible for the different parties involved in creating AI-generated works to qualify as authors under the law, with the economic and moral rights attributed accordingly. However, I also argue that this is an impractical solution for a few different reasons. Primarily, however, is the fact that both the act of creating the software and its operation for the purpose of producing an AI-generated work generally involves a large cast of stakeholders whose composition radically shifts on a case-by-case basis. Given this variability, determining a legal rule or administrative policy that can be consistently applied across all cases equitably would be impractical. As such, this chapter concludes that other mechanisms for assigning copyright or similar rights in AI-generated works should be developed moving forward.

4.2 Overview of Indonesian and EU Copyright Law

Copyright law generally sets three main requirements for granting copyright protection for literary and artistic works, namely that they are 1) fixed into a material form; 2) created by an author or authors; and 3) original. When those requirements are fulfilled, the author is entitled to copyright, which gives rise to economic and moral rights. The discussion in this section is comprised of two sub-sections. The first analyses how AI-generated works challenge the current copyright requirements. The second discusses how moral and economic rights might be best understood in the case of AI-generated works and how and who they might be awarded.

4.2.1 Copyright Protection Requirements

In the EU, copyright protection necessitates that the works be original, created by an author, and fixed in a tangible medium of expression.[3] These requirements are slightly different from the Indonesian Copyright Act (hereinafter, the Act) which stipulates that a work must 1) have a fixed form, 2) be created by an author, and 3)

[3] Copyright in the EU is a collection of national laws, see Hutukka 2023, p. 1051.

result from thought or creativity.[4] Indonesia does not require works to be original its copyright law also protects traditional cultural expressions, whose production requires copying and modifying existing expressions. In the context of AI-generated works, the central challenges for attracting copyright protection that are raised under the Act relate to the authorship requirement, as detailed in Sect. 5.2.2, and what is termed the creativity requirement, as detailed in Sect. 5.2.3.

4.2.2 Authorship

The EU does not have a widely-accepted consensus as to who an author is, and leaves the definition of an author to the national laws of its Member States. [5] The EU's Computer Program Directive establishes that the author should be a natural person.[6] However, it also gives discretionary power to its Member States to regard a legal person, such as company, as an author.[7] Similarly, Indonesian copyright law sets that an author needs to 1) be a legal person, who 2) exercises creativity or intellectual effort in creating works. It defines an author as 'a person or a group of persons, who either individually or jointly produce works that are distinctive and personal'.[8] A person is defined in the Copyright Act to include legal persons, which enables corporations to receive copyright over a work. Generative AI, a computer program which plays a central role in producing AI-generated works, can neither be regarded as a natural person nor a legal person. If we consider generative AI as the sole creator of these works, they cannot receive copyright protection because their creator fails to fulfil the authorship requirements of copyright law.

Both Indonesian and EU copyright law imply a personality requirement, which necessitates that the author's personality should be reflected in the work.[9] The requirements of personality are often seen as a major challenge to copyright protection for AI-generated works. There are doubts about whether generative AI can 'reflect personality' owing to the mechanical nature of its operation. To satisfy this requirement it must be shown that the work results from the author's mind. In the case of AI-generated works, this requires a direct relationship between human authors and the AI-generated works. This would be difficult to show when human authors contribute little to the resulting work. Another potential problem is that an author must have knowledge of how the work was created. In the case of AI-generated

[4] Article 1(1)–(3), *Law number 28 of 2014 on Copyright 2014 (Indonesia)* (2014 Copyright Act).

[5] Phillips 2008, p. 794.

[6] Article 2 (1), *Directive 2009/24/EC of the European Parliament and the Council of 23 April 2009 on the legal protection of computer programs* (Computer Program Directive).

[7] Ibid.

[8] Article 1(2), 2014 Copyright Act, above n. 4.

[9] Ibid.

works, this would be difficult to prove because more often than not generative AI operate as black boxes.[10]

While at first blush the personality requirement may suggest that AI-generated works would be unable to be protected by copyright, the situation may change if we look more closely at how generative AI operates in practice. In some cases, for example, generative AI may be used to support human authors to produce works in a more efficient manner. In these situations, a human author who collaborates with generative AI could be considered to be an author who bears a legal personality status. When generative AI and an Indonesian scarf designer collaborate, for example, the personality requirement is met by the designer's contribution to the creation of the scarf through the selection of a pattern and the fixation of that pattern in particular textile. This can be further supported by the fact that the scarf is produced by the designer's mind and that the designer has the expertise and ability to create the scarf.

Another situation where AI-generated works may be able to satisfy the personality requirement is where a collective of authors designs and trains generative AI to produce works which are subsequently commercialised by the collective (as with *Obvious AI)*.[11] In this scenario, the authors involved in the collective could possibly be regarded as authors of the resulting work because they meet the legal personhood requirement. However, they could possibly fail to meet the personality requirement because the work is directly produced by generative AI, thus eliminating the direct link between the authors and the work.[12]

In other situations, generative AI can produce high-quality works without much intervention from human authors. As discussed in Chap. 2, it is possible for generative AI (such as *ChatGPT*, *DALL-E*, or *AIVA)* to create works with little human contribution because the role of the human user is only to prompt the generative AI to create works, for example by typing a line of command and pressing the 'enter' button. In this situation, even though human users can fulfil the legal personhood requirement, they may not be able to fulfil the personality requirement because they cannot show how their personality reflects in the AI-generated works.

4.2.3 Originality/Creativity

4.2.3.1 The Concept of Originality

The originality requirements can be found in the 2002 Indonesian Copyright Act. It was no longer required through the 2014 Copyright Act along with the inclusion of traditional cultural expressions as one of its subject matters of protection. Some

---

[10] Deeks 2019, p. 1829.

[11] Obvious AI is an art collective that develops generative AI to produce paintings.

[12] In general, the human brain processes analogue data continuously, while a computer processes digital data in a binary manner (Huson 2018, pp. 57–58). Further debate on the computer's 'mind' can be found in Samuelson 1986 and Butler 1982.

traditional cultural expressions in Indonesia are made by way of copying and modifying previous expressions, making it unable to meet the originality requirement. In the EU, a copyright-protected work should meet the originality requirement, which means that the work should be the author's own intellectual creation,[13] and be the expression of the author's personality.[14]

In the EU, the concept of originality is often related to personality requirement.[15] For example, in the *Infopaq* case, the court understood that an author's intellectual creation is evident through their expression of creativity in an original manner.[16] A work is considered original as long as it is created by its author, and not copied.[17] Further, in the *Painer* case, CJEU emphasised that the work is original if it involves the authors' personal and creative choices.[18] The *Painer* case, which concerns photograph as a subject matter, affirms that a photograph can demonstrate the author's personal and creative choices. The photographer has free choices in arranging the lighting and angle of the photographed object. This case can be relevant to the generative AI problems because both concerns work created with the aid of a machine.

As explained in Chap. 2 of this book, the making of AI-generated works requires human contributions. Assessing human's involvement in the making of AI-generated works could help us understand whether the works meet copyright's originality requirement. In a partially-generative AI,[19] where the contributions of both the generative AI and users are equally balanced, originality subsists in the user's personal and creative choices in editing, finalising, and selecting the works. The real challenge lies with fully-generative-AI, a type of AI where users have minimal contribution. Originality may not be present in this type of AI because the decisions are primarily made by the algorithm, leaving no opportunity for the authors to express their personal and creative choices into the works.

4.2.3.2 Creativity Requirement in Indonesia

For a work to be protected by copyright in Indonesia, it must be the product of inspiration, ability, thought, imagination, dexterity, skill or expertise expressed in a tangible form.[20] That is, to be protected a work must be an 'intellectual creation', that involves creative activity as an expression of a human's mind.[21] Although not mentioned explicitly in the Act, it suggests that human authorship is required. In a

---

13 *Case C-310/17 Levola Hengelo [2018] ECLI:EU:C:2018:618*, para 36.

14 Ibid., para 37.

15 Rosati 2013.

16 *Case C-5/08 Infopaq International [2009] ECR I-6569*, para 11.

17 Ibid.

18 *Case C-145/10 Painer v. Standard VerlagsGmbH, 2011 E.C.R. I-1254*, para 89.

19 Ginsburg and Budiardjo 2019, pp. 375–377.

20 Article 1(3), 2014 Copyright Act, above n. 4.

21 Antons 2000, p. 58.

way, creativity is required to distinguish between human and non-human artefacts.[22] This implies that copyright only protects the product of human creativity.

Unlike the personality requirement, which necessitates certain conditions to be met, the creativity requirements are rarely, if ever, discussed in case law.[23] Creativity is mostly assumed to be present without the parties having to prove its existence. Instead, the courts tend to rely on the personality requirement that demands an author to be connected to his/her work.

This lack of discussion suggests that the effort required to demonstrate that the work was produced through creativity is quite low. Following this suggestion, it is possible that an AI-generated work may meet this low threshold. One other possibility is to consider the users' creativity in producing AI-generated works. The creativity of users is often questioned because a generative AI's capacity to create works autonomously relegate the users' role and creativity to a minimum.[24] However, taking into account that the creativity threshold is low, the users' contribution, no matter how small, can be presumed to exist in AI-generated works.

A further possibility is that generative AI can be considered independently creative. To support this argument, Annemarie Bridy argues that if a human author needs to demonstrate only a low standard of creativity, why should a computer (program) as author be required to meet a higher standard?[25] Further, Bridy discusses human and computer creativity by asserting that if creativity is understood as human consciousness, software will never be regarded as creative; but if creativity is understood as the ability to do something unpredictable beyond the established-rule, it may have the chance to be regarded as creative.[26]

It is also possible that AI-generated works will fulfil the creativity need under copyright law because the work created is unpredictable. As discussed in Chap. 2, the production of AI-generated work involves 'playing with the data' and the 'running model' stages. In the former, software developers and data analysts/trainers use training data to train generative AI algorithm to create new patterns. Meanwhile in the latter, the algorithm is already capable of creating new patterns by itself. During

---

[22] Jened 2014, p. 88.

[23] The author's creativity is almost always automatically assumed in the court decisions because both a copyright infringement and a copyright dispute deal with human authorship; there has so far been no case dealing with non-human authorship in Indonesia.

[24] In his article, Robert Yu argues that there is a different level of creativity between the users of generative AI software and the users of a camera. Camera users are still required to decide the photograph's composition, angle, and many other elements while the users of generative AI software generally need only to press 'enter' to execute the software (see Yu 2017).

[25] The context of creativity discussed in Bridy's publication focuses mainly on the United States creativity requirement in its copyright law. Bridy asserts that even though the United States copyright law requires a particular standard of creativity in its early decision, such as in the *Trademark* case and *Burrow-Giles,* the development of the creativity requirement diminished as a consequence of the decision in the *Feist* case, where the judges decided that arranging names based on their alphabetical order does not require creativity. Bridy argues that this decision shows more of what creativity *is not* rather than what it is. Soon after, more court decisions referring to *Feist* exhausted the concept of creativity in Bridy 2012, p. 282.

[26] Ibid.

the 'running model' stage, even the programmers and data trainers cannot predict the outcome of the generative AI. The software runs autonomously at this second stage, so this is where it is unpredictable. If unpredictability is what is required to prove creativity, the software can be creative in producing AI-generated works.

4.3 Economic Rights and Moral Rights

Both Indonesian and EU copyright grants economic and moral rights to an author of a protected work. Moral rights deal with the author's right to be acknowledged as the author of the work and/or to modify the work. Moral rights stay with the author of the work and cannot be transferred to anyone else. Alternatively, economic rights give rights to the author to benefit from the use of his/her work. Unlike moral rights that are not transferrable, economic rights can be transferred to other parties. Copyright will only transfer the economic rights of the author to another party but not the moral rights. For example, when a programmer transfers his economic rights of a photo-editing software to a software company, the software company has the right to copy and distribute the software. However, the software company would not have the rights to either change the code in the software or omit the programmer's name as the author of the software.

As creating AI-generated works involves multiple actors who might potentially be considered to have authorial input, including the software, questions arise about how to allocate the economic and moral rights.

4.3.1 Economic Rights

Economic rights are the author's or the copyright holder's exclusive rights to gain economic benefit arising out of the work.[27] This includes the rights to publish, reproduce, translate, adapt, arrange, transform, distribute, perform, communicate and rent the works.[28] In general, only authors as copyright holders, are allowed to perform their economic rights and also have the rights to prohibit others from assessing such rights without their consent.[29]

The duration of protection for economic rights conferred by the Indonesian Copyright Act differs depending on the type of work. Overall, the act provides for three different lengths of duration in the following manner:

i) Literary and artistic works, in the form of books, pamphlets, speeches, lectures, educational aids, songs, dramatic works, dances, choreography, puppet shows,

[27] Article 8(f), 2014 Copyright Act, above n. 4.

[28] Article 9(1), Ibid.

[29] Article 9(3), Ibid.

pantomimes, fine artworks, architectural works, maps and batik products are protected for up to 70 years after the death of the author.[30]

ii) Photographic and cinematographic works, computer programs, and databases are protected for 50 years after it is first made available to the public.[31]

iii) Works of applied arts[32] are protected for 25 years after its it is firstly made available to the public.[33]

The philosophical justification for economic rights is commonly attributed to Locke's theory of labour. He asserts that economic rights are given to a property owner to reward 'the unpleasantness' of labour. In the case of a copyright owner, this applies to the author whose unpleasant labour produced the work.[34] This unpleasantness could typically be understood as the time spent to create the work and the cost the author bears in creating it. In other words, the author deserves to be given copyright to compensate for his/her sacrifices made to produce the work.

Copyright gives monopoly-like rights to copyright holder.[35] This monopolistic nature allows an author (or copyright holder) to exploit his/her work while simultaneously excluding others from exploiting it. The protection is important because the cost of creating works is often high, while the cost of copying works is generally low.[36] Without being able to hold monopoly rights over their work, the authors may find their economic returns too small to cover the cost of creating it,[37] thus consequently being discouraged from doing so.[38] That is, protection is granted as an incentive for authors to produce more works in the future.[39]

In analysing who should be awarded economic rights in AI-generated works, I need to assess which parties, among software developers, data trainers, users, and software, may have the greatest interests over such compensation and incentive. In doing so, I consider which of these parties have gone through the unpleasantness of labour and need to be rewarded with monopoly rights.

---

[30] Article 58(1), Ibid.

[31] Article 59(1), Ibid.

[32] Applied arts comprise industrial design, graphic design, fashion design, interior design and decorative art (in Panofsky et al. 1955).

[33] Article 59 (2), 2014 Copyright Act, above n. 4.

[34] Hughes 1988.

[35] Miller 1993.

[36] Landes and Posner 1989.

[37] Yen 1990, p. 518.

[38] Even though it is often argued that monopoly rights incentivise the authors to create more works, it might not be the only reason. Nina I. Brown asserts that authors may be motivated by the urges for self-development, personal satisfaction, and a desire to challenge oneself, see Brown 2018.

[39] Hughes 1988.

4.3.1.1 Potential Parties Eligible for Economic Rights in AI-generated Works

In the early development of AI, creating AI-generated works relied heavily on what humans had contributed because software was not as independent as it is today. During this early period, the software user was presumed to be author and, by extension, also the copyright holder, in relation to AI-generated works.[40] Given recent technological advances, generative AI is able to be more autonomous in the sense that it can create AI-generated works with negligible human intervention. Furthermore, the capacity of generative AI to act independently is expected to expand. The emerging autonomous capability of generative AI challenges copyright law about whether it can and should be the author of the work and thus eligible for the economic rights. Another possibility is that software developers and software users hold the economic rights over AI-generated works.

The first possibility is to grant the economic rights to the software developers and/or data trainers because they have created the software by determining the software's function and underlying algorithms, generating the code, training the software, and resolving bugs arising within the process.[41] While Locke's labour theory talks about the 'unpleasantness' of this labour requiring compensation, programmers have already been compensated by the copyright they have over the software code itself, thus indicating that granting economic rights to the programmer would over-reward them.[42] This line of argument also applies when we try to justify software developers' rights to protection over the AI-generated works, since they only bear the cost of producing the generative AI not the AI-generated works. Therefore, while copyright would give them rights over the generative AI to offset the costs they have borne in producing the software, it is hard to justify software developers' economic rights over the AI-generated works because they may bear low to no costs of production.

The second option is to grant economic rights to the generative AI user, which may be possible, depending on the user's role in creating AI-generated works. Jane Ginsburg and Luke Budiardjo classify three spectrums of generative software, namely, 1) ordinary tools, in which the end results depend highly on the users' contribution; 2) partially-generative, in which the end results reflect both the programmers and the users' contribution; and 3) fully-generative, in which the end results depend only on the programmers' contribution.[43] Based on these classifications, the software users may obtain economic rights of AI-generated works only when they contribute their labour to the work. Consequently, in the sense that the software is fully generative, and the users' role is restricted to executing the program, they may not be entitled to economic rights.

---

[40] Samuelson 1986.

[41] Yu 2017.

[42] Ibid.

[43] Ginsburg and Budiardjo 2019, pp. 405–407.

It is also important to assess whether the users need the rights over the AI-generated works,[44] since the users notably select and publish the resulting work, which often requires them to finance the process. The result of my fieldwork shows that the users' roles are not restricted to executing the generative AI. In the collaboration between Indonesian scarf designer and *Rinna* AI, for example, the designer selects the most-suitable AI-generated patterns, applies the patterns to fabric, and sells the scarves. Because all those procedures attract a cost that needs to be borne by the users, giving them economic rights to cover that cost is justifiable.

The third and least-likely option is to award economic rights to the generative AI itself. Although AI-generated works are generated by code, attributing economic rights to software would be problematic primarily because a computer program is not a legal entity[45] and because it lacks the capacity to manage and defend the economic benefit arising out of its creation. Moreover, in creating things, software does not perform labour that needs to be compensated, nor does it need monopoly rights to incentivise the creation of more works. As generative AI generally creates works whenever the user tells it to do so, granting economic rights to the generative AI may be the least-preferred option.

4.3.2 Moral Rights

In contrast to economic rights that can be transferred to other parties, Indonesian and EU copyright law treats moral rights as being inherent to the author of the work. Moral rights in Indonesia were directly inherited from Dutch law during the colonial era with that system incorporating the French's *droit moral* commonly found in legal systems throughout continental Europe. The Dutch adopted moral rights in the early 19th century when France annexed the Dutch kingdom.[46] Moral rights were then passed to Indonesia through the Dutch colonial 1912 Copyright Act. In theory, the 1912 Copyright Act remained in force until Indonesia instituted its own copyright law in 1982;[47] but, in reality, it was modestly enforced during the early-Independence era.[48]

Moral rights in France can be traced back to the late 18th century. Before this period, copyright only protected the economic rights of the authors and/or

---

[44] See Samuelson 1986 and Yu 2017.

[45] Bridy 2012, p. 21.

[46] Saunders 1992, p. 75.

[47] Upon its independence, Indonesia's 1945 Constitution indicated that any colonial laws and regulations were still in force until replaced with new national laws and regulations. Therefore, the 1912 Dutch Copyright Act was still applicable for Indonesia until it adopted its own national copyright law in 1982.

[48] During 1945–1982, the Indonesian government wanted its people to copy foreign books freely to support their education. This was the reason why, at this period of time, Indonesia was reluctant to grant copyright protection for foreign works and only protected domestic authors' works.

publishers.[49] In the late 18th century, however, the notion of romantic authorship influenced the way moral rights protection developed.[50] It gave inalienable rights to the author over his/her works because he/she was seen as an 'independent original genius' who creates works out of his/her personality.[51] In doing so, a strong connection between an author and his work is established that is honoured through moral rights. In contrast to economic rights, which an author may sell or rent to other parties, moral rights remain with the author: they are inalienable throughout his/her lifetime and may pass through his/her estate after death.[52] [53] Moral rights grant authors the entitlement to attribution and integrity. The right of attribution means that an author is entitled to choose if his/her name or pseudonym is mentioned or not mentioned when the work is used.[54] Conversely, the right of integrity ensures that the author is entitled to alter his/her work, including title and sub-title of the work, and to prevent the work being distorted, mutilated, modified, or subject to any act that jeopardises the author's dignity or reputation.[55] Moral rights, along with economic rights, end once copyright protection expires.[56]

The moral rights in the 2014 Indonesia Copyright Act are similar to the Dutch Copyright Act. However, the latter also grant rights to the author to resist publication of his work when either 1) his name is not mentioned in the work; or 2) a name other than his is mentioned in the work.[57] Furthermore, the Dutch Copyright Act also limits moral rights by the test of reasonableness,[58] and provides that modifications made in good faith, and in accordance with social custom, do not infringe moral rights (e.g., typographic errors).[59] Pointedly, this test is not acknowledged in Indonesian copyright law.

Moral rights become one of the most challenging and complex domains when we consider the topic of copyright and AI-generated works. Traditionally, moral rights

---

[49] In the 15th–16th century, the right to publish works (book-privilege) was vested in the king. When an author or a publisher wished to publish their works, they needed to obtain permission from the King. Once granted, they would have the rights to publish the works for an initial ten-year duration that could, upon application, be extended for a further ten years. Upon its appearance, the book-privilege protected the authors or the publishers' economic interests against the unauthorized reprinters; it was not until the 17th century that the book-privilege was directed at controlling the circulation of works that might contain critical messages regarding the kingdom (Saunders 1992).

[50] Rajan 2011, p. 7.

[51] Ibid.

[52] This notion was clearly depicted in the *Marquam C. Lehuby* case where Marquam, an author of children's textbooks, sold his books directly to Lehuby, a bookseller. The bookseller altered the books by taking out forty to fifty pages so that they would be more acceptable for use in Catholic schools. The Trial Court of Paris decided that the bookseller's action might jeopardize the author's reputation and thus they should be returned to their original form (Peeler 1999, p. 448).

[53] Article 5(2) and (3), 2014 Copyright Act, above n. 4.

[54] Article 57, Ibid.

[55] Article 5 (1), Ibid.

[56] Article 57, Ibid.

[57] Article 35(1)(a)–(b), Dutch Copyright Law, in van Eechoud and Cohen Jehoram 1993.

[58] Ibid.

[59] Geller et al. 1993.

are heavily rooted in the *droit d'auteur* tradition that is derived from the notion that there is an inseparable connection between an author's personality and theirs works.[60] However, given that the production of AI-generated works might involve multiple parties with significantly different roles, establishing such a connection is not necessarily simple nor automatic, nor is it necessarily clear that such a connection might even exist.

There are a number of reasons for this. First, highly sophisticated generative AI software may be considered to be an author on the basis that it produces the AI-generated works autonomously and without any human intervention.[61] As the work is created by the software, there is a direct author-work connection in terms of the relationship of the software and the AI-generated works. The downside of this argument is that the software's ability to produce works may not correspond with its personality in the work.

Establishing moral rights requires a higher threshold than merely producing the work, namely that the personality of the author is reflected in the work.[62] If personality is perceived as a distinctive feature of an author's mental state that is neither alienable nor exists in other authors',[63] generative AI cannot demonstrate its own personality. This is because the software's ability to generate different patterns or genres of works solely depends on the data provided by the data trainer. The software, no matter how autonomous, only generates works according to the patterns it has learnt from the training, that is, different training data may influence the software to generate different genres of works.[64] Therefore, I contend that the training data determine the software's ability, which can be alienated to other generative AI if given similar training data. This alienable nature could not be deemed personality, but merely reflect the software's artificial propensity. If the software's personality is not reflected in the work, moral rights cannot be attributed to generative AI.

In Indonesia, personality is measured in the way that 1) a work is made by the author; and 2) the author knows how to make the work.[65] These standards open the possibility for the law to recognise that the personality of generative AI is reflected in the works it produces.[66] The first requirement can be easily met because AI-generated works are made by generative AI. The challenge is the second requirement, that is the need to show how the software generates works. The problem here is even though it is clear how the AI-generated works are produced, the software and the people who work behind it may be unable to explain how the works are created. The problem is that the technology is black-boxed, by which the generative AI algorithm develops

---

[60] Lim 2018.

[61] Miernicki and Ng 2020, p. 4.

[62] Yanisky-Ravid and Martens 2019, p. 143.

[63] Biron 2014, p. 27.

[64] Lehr and Ohm 2017, p. 680.

[65] *Republic of Indonesia v. Arifin No 35/Pid.Sus/2016/PN/Yyk.*

[66] This argument assumes that an author could be anyone and is not limited by the requirement of legal personality.

into a complex structure in that even its initial programmers may not understand how it works.[67]

The second option is to attribute moral rights to the humans involved in creating AI-generated works. This could include software developers, data trainers, or its users. While these parties will have their own personality, that is, an inalienable mental state, which that exists innately within themselves, it is unclear whether this personality would be reflected in the work.[68] Moreover, while the personality of software developers who create generative AI may be reflected in the software, this does not necessarily mean that their personality is also reflected in the resulting AI-generated works because the software makes its own independent choices when generating the work.[69] Meanwhile, the data trainers who collect, review, and train data for the software[70] may be important in determining the software's ability to generate AI-generated works. During the training, the data trainers provide large amounts of data to the software, teach it to reach a desirable outcome, and eliminate undesirable ones.[71] Such training constructs and sharpens the generative AI software's ability to recognise patterns and independently create works based on them.[72] Still, the personality of the data trainers may not be reflected in the works because they have not created the training data. Rather the software independently creates AI-generated works. In this regard, the data trainers are analogous to a teacher who tells students how to create a work: while they may influence their creation, their personality will not be reflected in the students' works. Similarly, it is unlikely that the personality of software users will be reflected in the AI-generated works because their role is usually restricted to executing the software and not to making a creative contribution.[73]

Even though the most probable argument is to bestow moral rights to the generative AI, the problem remains that moral rights describe an important authorial entitlement and Indonesian copyright law restricts the definition of an author to natural and legal persons. This creates problems for recognising software's moral rights as it does not qualify as a 'person' under Indonesian copyright law. Thus, it may be necessary to re-think of the possibility of multiple authorship to protect AI-generated works.

---

[67] Rich 2016, p. 886.

[68] Further investigation on the human role in the creation of CGW will be conducted at the field research stage.

[69] Bridy 2012.

[70] Lehr and Ohm 2017.

[71] Yanisky-Ravid and Hallisey 2019, p. 439.

[72] Ibid.

[73] Miernicki and Ng 2020.

4.4 Conclusion

Contemporary Indonesian copyright law tends to be similar to many European countries, in so far as it protects the moral rights of authors, where the author is seen as an independent original genius whose personality is reflected in his/her work. Similarly, the authorship/personality requirement also reflects the influence of Dutch law which believes that the author connects strongly to his/her work. For AI-generated works, making this connection is challenging for two reasons. First, multiple parties are involved in the creation of AI-generated works. Second, AI-generated works are generated autonomously by AI software. While, from this perspective, a case can be made for software to be recognised as the author of the AI-generated works because legal personality is absent, the software cannot be considered as an author under Indonesian copyright law.

AI-generated works provide direct challenges to copyright law's authorship and creativity requirements. The authorship requirement is central to this discussion because creating AI-generated works involves multiple parties performing different roles. The need for creativity is also challenging because it can only be fulfilled by a human author, though at present, the software may demonstrate similar creativity to that of a human author. The discussion in this chapter examined the possibility of granting copyright to the parties involved in creating AI-generated works, such as computer programmers, software users, data trainers, and even through the software itself. It showed that software's users may be granted copyright on the condition that they also contribute to the process. Additionally, it showed that copyright may be attributed to programmers who have designed and resolved issues arising in the generative AI software, and that programmer may be eligible for copyright protection if their personality is reflected in the AI-generated works and they can show that how they contribute to developing generative AI is equivalent to the intellectual/creative efforts within the AI-generated works. Meanwhile, this chapter found that there is little potential for software to be considered as the copyright owner of AI-generated works. The reason for this was that as a computer program lacks legal personhood, it would prevent the software from exercising the associated economic rights.

References

Antons C (2000) Intellectual Property Law in Indonesia. Kluwer Law International, The Netherlands

Biron L (2014) Creative work and communicative norms. In: van Eechoud M (ed) The Work of Authorship. Amsterdam University Press, Amsterdam, pp 19–44. https://doi.org/10.1515/9789048523009-002

Bridy A (2012) Coding Creativity: Copyright and the Artificially Intelligent Author. Stanford Technology Law Review 5:1–28

Brown N I (2018) Artificial Authors: A Case for Copyright in Computer-Generated Works. The Columbia Science and Technology Law Review 20:1–41. https://doi.org/10.7916/stlr.v20i1.4766

Butler T L (1982) Can a Computer be an Author? – Copyright Aspects of Artificial Intelligence. Hastings Communications and Entertainment Law Journal 4(4):707–747

Deeks A (2019) The Judicial Demand for Explainable Artificial Intelligence. Columbia Law Review 119(7):1829–1850

Geller P E et al. (eds) (1993) International copyright law and practice. Matthew Bender, New York

Ginsburg J C, Budiardjo L A (2019) Authors and Machines. Berkeley Technology Law Journal 34(2):343–448

Hughes J (1988) The Philosophy of Intellectual Property. Georgetown Law Journal 77(2):287

Huson G (2018) I, Copyright. Santa Clara High Technology Law Journal 35(2):54–78

Hutukka P (2023) Copyright Law in the European Union, the United States and China. IIC—International Review of Intellectual Property and Competition Law 54(7):1044–1080. https://doi.org/10.1007/s40319-023-01357-0

Jened R (2014) Hukum Hak Cipta [Copyright Law]. Citra Aditya Bakti, Bandung

Landes W M, Posner R A (1989) An economic analysis of copyright law. The Journal of Legal Studies 18(2): 325–363

Lehr D, Ohm P (2017) Playing with the Data: What Legal Scholars Should Learn About Machine Learning. UC Davis Law Review 51:653–717

Lim D (2018) AI & IP: Innovation & Creativity in an Age of Accelerated Change. Akron Law Review 52:813–875

Lukman J (2019) AI & modest wear: Ria Miranda celebrates 10-year fashion career. The Jakarta Post. https://www.thejakartapost.com/news/2019/11/30/ai-modest-wear-ria-miranda-celebrates-10-year-fashion-career.html. Accessed 4 February 2020

Miernicki M, Ng I (2020) Artificial intelligence and moral rights. AI & SOCIETY 36(1):319–329. https://doi.org/10.1007/s00146-020-01027-6

Miller A R (1993) Copyright Protection for Computer Programs, Databases, and Computer-Generated Works: Is Anything New Since CONTU? Harvard Law Review 106(5):977–1073. https://doi.org/10.2307/1341682

Panofsky E et al. (1955) Meaning in the visual arts: papers in and on art history, Vol 39. Doubleday Garden City, New York

Peeler C D (1999) From the Providence of Kings to Copyrighted Things (and French Moral Rights). Indiana International & Comparative Law Review 9(2):423–456. https://doi.org/10.18060/17468

Phillips J (2008) Authorship, ownership, wikiship: copyright in the twenty-first century. Journal of intellectual property law & practice 3(12):788–798. https://doi.org/10.1093/jiplp/jpn200

Rajan M T S (2011) Moral Rights: Principles, Practice and New Technology. Oxford University Press, New York. https://doi.org/10.1093/acprof:osobl/9780195390315.001.0001

Rich M L (2016) Machine Learning, Automated Suspicion Algorithms, and the Fourth Amendment. University of Pennsylvania Law Review 164(4):871–929

Rosati E (2013) Originality in EU Copyright: Full Harmonization through Case Law, 1st edn. Edward Elgar Publishing, Cheltenham

Samuelson P (1986) Allocating Ownership Rights in Computer-Generated Works. University of Pittsburgh Law Review 47:1185–1228

Saunders D (1992) Authorship and copyright. Routledge Revivals

van Eechoud M, Cohen Jehoram H (1993) Netherlands. In: Geller PE et al. (eds) International copyright law and practice. Matthew Bender, New York

Yanisky-Ravid S, Hallisey S K (2019) Equality and Privacy by Design: A New Model of Artificial Intelligence Data Transparency via Auditing, Certification, and Safe Harbor Regimes. Fordham Urban Law Journal 46(2):428–486

Yanisky-Ravid S, Martens C (2019) From the Myth of Babel to Google Translate: Confronting Malicious Use of Artificial Intelligence – Copyright and Algorithmic Biases in Online Translations Systems. Seattle University Law Review 43(1):99–168

Yen A C (1990) Restoring the natural law: Copyright as labor and possession. Ohio State Law Journal 51:517–559

Yu R (2017) The machine author: what level of copyright protection is appropriate for fully independent computer-generated works? University of Pennsylvania Law Review 165(5):1245–1270

Chapter 5
AI-generated Works and the Notion of Authorship

Contents

Abstract Authorship is one of the fundamental requirements within copyright protection. At the same time, it is the primary reason AI-generated works cannot be protected under current copyright laws. This chapter explores the development of the concept of authorship and tries to answer how it may need to adapt to accommodate generative AI. It begins by examining the history of authorship in Europe, detailing its shift from prioritising publishers to valuing authors' interests, and the subsequent criticism of the notion of romantic authorship. The chapter highlights the challenge generative AI poses to traditional authorship, as romantic authorship typically protects a limited number of authors, while AI-generated works often involve multiple contributors, including the software. This complexity points out the inadequacy of the romantic author concept in reflecting modern creative practices. Generative AI, along with other collaborative forms of creation, underscores the need for a redefined and more inclusive framework of authorship to accommodate the challenges brought by generative AI and collaborative creation.

Keyword Authorship · Hyper-authorship · Romantic author · Postmodern copyright · Generative AI · Collective authorship · Creative practices

L. Andrini, *Protecting Artificial Intelligence-generated Works in Indonesia*, Information Technology and Law Series 41, https://doi.org/10.1007/978-94-6265-703-8_5

5.1 Introduction

Obvious, a French based collective of software developers and artists work together to develop and produce new works of art. To do this, the collective develops the requisite code, collects training data from 18th century artworks, and uses these resources to produce AI models capable of generating realistic portraits that have the qualities of museum-displayed artworks. One of the AI-produced paintings, *Le Comte de Belamy*, was sold at an auction at Christie's in 2018 for almost US$500,000. The *Obvious* collective offers an example of the creation of AI-generated works that requires contributions from multiple parties who work as a single entity. It also demonstrates that human involvement in developing code, collecting data, and training the generative AI is required to enable the creation of these AI-generated works. Moreover, it also demonstrates that such works can attract significant commercial and cultural value—as demonstrated in the sale price that *Le Comte de Belamy* attracted in an esteemed art venue.

The definition of authorship under copyright law, especially as it is tied to the notion of romantic authorship, imagines an ability to easily identify a discrete author or set of authors involved in the creation of the work and then, remunerate those individuals. However, when a work is produced through a collaboration involving numerous people, at some point, the number of authors can become too large to manage, in particular if there is not a clear organisational mechanism such as the *Obvious* collective. Moving from the arts to the sciences there are numerous examples of large-scale collaborations producing hyper-authored publications in academic scientific publishing. For example, in 2016, a team of researchers responsible for a general-purpose particle physics experiment at the European Council for Nuclear Research (CERN) published an article co-authored by 5,000 authors.[1] Similarly, in 2023, another article published on the modelling of a SARS-CoV-2 vaccination for surgery listed 15,025 separate co-authors.[2] With such a large number of authors, it becomes impossible to identify and reward the specific contribution of each individual involved in the creation.[3] This also has flow on implications for the ability of such a large group to manage copyright interests—obtaining agreements about how the collaboration can authorise the use, rent or sale of the protected work. Furthermore, it would also be absurd to hold either a particular individual or the authorial team, as a whole, accountable for such hyper-authored works in the event that the scientific integrity of the underlying research be questioned.[4] As a result, the notion of authorship in a hyper-authored works often becomes, in effect, meaningless. While there are numerous examples of this issue in academic science, generative AI systems and AI-generated works can, in many cases, present similar issues in that there are numerous stakeholders involved in their creation.

---

[1] Nature Index 2018.

[2] Nogrady 2023.

[3] Cronin 2001, p. 562.

[4] Ibid.

While contemporary creative works often demonstrate hyper-authorship,[5] copyright necessitates a limited number of authors for practically managing and distributing rights. Simply put, the authors and their inputs are difficult to count, evaluate, and reward with rights. This means that at some point, an artificial line needs to be drawn between inspiration and actual input in the work. In the music industry, for example, the practice of sampling (i.e., reusing a portion of an existing sound recording), shows that new works are often inspired by previous ones. Some cases in the United States have demonstrated that it is possible to cut the link between inspiration and actual input into the work. In *Bridgeport Music Inc. v. Dimension Films*, for example, Bridgeport Music sued NWA for sampling and manipulating three notes from George Clinton's "Get Off Your Ass and Jam", a song to which the holding company owned the rights.[6] In this situation, the Court could have decided that NWA's sampling might have been exempted through fair use and/or the *de minimis* rule—indicating the presence of a technical copyright violation, but one whose effect was insignificant. However, the Court did not do this and, instead, took a more literal approach that emphasised sampling, no matter how small or seemingly insignificant, violated copyright. This decision is problematic not only for creative practices that involve sampling, such as hip-hop music, mosaic, or bricolage, but also for the creation of AI-generated works—which also have numerous stakeholders whose input is reflected in the work.

AI and its ability to generate works demands that the notion of romantic authorship be revisited for two reasons. First, creating AI-generated works involves numerous contributors and thus has the potential to be considered as hyper-authored works. It involves a significant number of programmers, data trainers, and users who want to be rewarded and recognised in the creation of works. Unfortunately, for reasons of simplicity, copyright often favours only acknowledging a limited number of authors. This requirement itself is problematic as it does not reflect the whole creative process and may leave the efforts of some contributors unrewarded. Second, creating AI-generated works uses a massive amount of existing works as training data to improve the ability and accuracy of AI algorithms. This often raises questions about whether the authors of those works need to be acknowledged as the authors of the AI-generated works.[7] This argument sees AI-generated works as combining inspiration and the actual input of the work, and thus demands copyright to separate the two.

In looking for the most suitable way to protect AI-generated works, my analysis considers multiple approaches to the notion of authorship, namely, both romantic and collective. To gain a better understanding of 'romantic authorship', in the first section of this chapter, I focus on what an 'author' means, how this has changed throughout European history, and how this has influenced the construction of authorship in Indonesia. In Europe, the earliest versions of copyright focused on protecting

---

[5] This term is borrowed from Blaise Cronin (in Cronin 2001).

[6] The song was written by George Clinton. Bridgeport Music Inc. owns the copyright of the song's recording.

[7] Rosati 2018.

publishers' interests by granting them monopoly rights.[8] At this time, authors did not take on special roles and thus received little to no privilege within the copyright system. Nonetheless, the focus changed during the era of the romantic author, when copyright law came to protect the interests of individual authors and glorified them as individual geniuses. Over time, copyright law's focus on the individual author was criticised mainly because the notion of romantic authorship restricted both copyright regulations and thus public access to knowledge. The idea of the romantic individual author is also considered to be problematic where the creative practices involve more than one author.[9] Despite such criticisms, romantic authorship still dominates in Indonesian copyright law.

The second section of the chapter focuses on the notion of authorship in Indonesian law and how it contrasts with Indonesian social norms and values. After providing an overview of the role and place of the author in Indonesian copyright law, I then look at the problems that arise in applying authorship to AI-generated works, which is one of the key reasons why traditional copyright law is not suitable to protect AI-generated works.

5.2 The Creation of AI-generated Works and the Challenges This Poses for Copyright Law

The way AI-generated works are created is subject to a common misconception. The popular belief is that the entire process of creation is automated and that human intervention is thus both unnecessary and irrelevant. As we saw earlier, creating AI-generated works involves at least three parties. First, software developers or programmers design and create machine learning algorithms. Second, data analyst/ data trainers collect, sort, arrange, and clean data to train the algorithm. Third, users operate and execute algorithms in a way that they can produce AI-generated works. In some cases, users also can play a role in preparing the AI-generated works for market. See also Fig. 5.1.

Technological developments that enable AI-generated works to be created challenge the current copyright system in at least two ways. First, they introduce multiple authors into the creative process, who have the potential to leave an imprint upon the AI-generated works and thus may be interested in becoming authors. Second, the involvement of generative AI software, which has a certain degree of autonomy, provokes a long-standing debate among copyright scholars about whether software can be considered an author.[10] In addressing these problems, this chapter shows how the notion of authorship has been modified to suit social changes. It further analyses

[8] The protection of publishers' rights through copyright happened both in the Anglo-Saxon and European continental countries, see Feather 1991; Grosheide 2010.

[9] See Woodmansee 1992.

[10] Some of the debate can be found in Samuelson 1986; Lim 2018; Huson 2018.

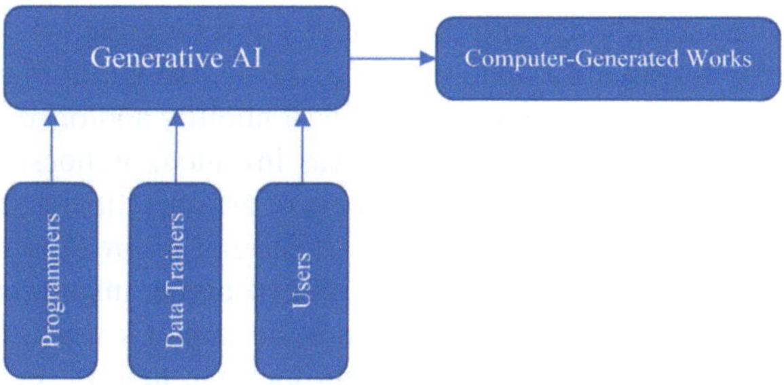

Fig. 5.1 The creation of computer-generated works *Source* The author

how authorship might be modified to answer the challenges posed by AI-generated works.

5.3 Development of the Concept of Authorship

The discussion of the early history of authorship focuses on the United Kingdom and European countries, where the practice and regulations on copyright have been accepted and have also influenced the creation of modern copyright law. A basic understanding of authorship in European countries is necessary to understand the shifting role of the author in modern global copyright law. This section of the chapter divides the European history of authorship into three periods. First, from the early inception of copyright, when authors' roles and entitlements were highlighted; second, the era of romantic authorship, when an author became the centre of copyright protection, and third, post-modern copyright, which focuses on the criticism of the concept of romantic authorship.

5.3.1 Authorship: From Guild System to Modern Copyright System

From the 12th century, many businesses in Europe and the United Kingdom were bound by guild-style regulations to control trades. A guild is typically a business organisation or league that operates according to a government licence[11] and is formed to reduce competition among its members, as well as gain collective political powers.[12] In pre-modern Europe, most guilds were generally organisations whose membership was limited to a trade or skill, such as that of weavers, bakers, armourers, jewellers and locksmiths.[13] During this period, guilds were authorised by local ruling

[11] Grosheide 2010.

[12] Ibid.

[13] Ibid.

elites (e.g., kings and the nobility) to set regulations to protect and restrict a particular artisanal occupation. In this sense, the guilds were powerful entities that often operated autonomously from local nobility and/or representatives of the king.

Before the printing press was invented, authors were not clearly distinguished from other types of craft workers or artisans. In this sense, both authors and artisans were seen more as messengers, instead of creators of works.[14] In large part, this distinction was based on the idea of divine inspiration—thus heavenly inspiration was believed to be the source of an author's work. In other words, the work was created by a celestial power through the help of an author who acted as an interpreter of the divine.[15] Other artisanal professions of this era, such as the illuminator of manuscripts, were also not seen as creating original works. Like the author, the role of the illuminator was considered more one of reproducing, copying, or modifying via divine inspiration.[16] Over time, the role of artisans such as the illuminator were replaced by the printing press, a machine that enabled manuscripts to be mass produced, yet the author remained. It was only after this occurred, that there was an increasing distinction between the creator of the work and the producer of its copies. As such, the printing press enabled the acknowledgement of the author as a distinct figure in the creation of a work.

The development and popularization of the printing press between 1450–1580 enabled the rapid diffusion of information and knowledge resources across countries. Initially, this proliferating diffusion caused uncertainty and suspicion amongst the elite and, as a result, attracted significant political attention and demanded legal oversight. In the Netherlands, for example, a publisher had to meet two requirements before they could produce and publicly distribute printed materials. First, the publisher had to obtain an exclusive license to publish from the central or local authorities. Second, the publisher had to ensure that the material was approved by a censorship authority.[17] A similar system operated in France, where the Crown granted an exclusive rights called printing privileges to authors and publishers, provided that they had obtained permission to publish from the Crown.[18] In England, printing privileges were introduced in 1518.[19] Through such privileges, a specific book should be licensed and registered on the Stationers' Company register before it could be published.[20] A book manuscript had to be licensed by official authorities with publishers being required to pay a registration fee before the manuscript could be listed on the Stationers' Company register.[21] According to Ronan Deazley,

[14] Ross 1994, pp. 234–237.
[15] Melton 2001, p. 82.
[16] Ibid.
[17] Melton 2001.
[18] Ginsburg 1989, p. 997.
[19] Dent 2014, p. 243.
[20] Ibid.
[21] Ibid.

this provided the Crown with an authority to "control the printing of seditious and heretical material."[22]

Regulations pertaining to book-selling at this time did not focus on author's rights. Instead, the privileges system in France, Netherlands and England were all introduced to protect the interests of book-sellers and governments.[23] For book-sellers, printing privileges gave publishers a monopoly over the sale of a particular book in the market. In contrast, for political authorities, printing privileges provided a means through which circulating texts could be controlled and liability for political seditious or socially offensive materials could be assigned.

Author's right came into consideration in the 18th century. In England, author's rights arose through the Statute of Anne (1710). The new law limited the term of protection to 14 years, with renewal possible for another 14 years, provided that the author was still alive.[24] The 1710 Act also established that the author was the original holder of the rights in their work.[25] The enclosure of author's rights in the Statute of Anne was arguably a strategy played by the Stationer's guild to hide its real intention to retain their monopoly over the book-selling businesses.[26]

Author's rights were first recognised in France in the 1793 copyright legislation,[27] mainly because recognising authors' rights was understood to promote public welfare.[28] In the Netherlands, the 1803 Copyright Act granted the drafter of a text a perpetual right to reproduce the text, though the primary right holder was the publisher. During the French annexation in 1810–1814, the French rule was introduced into the Netherlands. This gave authors an exclusive right to sell and distribute their works. However, after the French departure in 1814, this rule was withdrawn and the Netherlands' 1803 Copyright Act, which acknowledged the publisher's right to copy (*copyregt*), came back into effect. This remained the law in the Netherlands until the 1881 *Auteurswet* (translated as authors' rights) granted authors exclusive rights over their works. Indonesia inherited the Dutch 1912 Copyright Act during the period of colonialisation.

The legislation pertaining to copyright in the United Kingdom, France, and the Netherlands was similar in that it recognised the rights of authors. Despite these similarities, the legislation was created for different reasons. In the United Kingdom, the recognition of authors' rights was initially an extension of publishers' rights. It was also a mechanism that allowed the authorities to capture and assign individual responsibility for any treasonous content in manuscripts. Recognition of authors' rights in the Netherlands was largely influenced by the French idea of individual

---

[22] Deazley 2004, p. 2.

[23] Augustine Birrell explained that the printing privileges were generally granted to the booksellers, and only on rare occasions would they be granted to an individual author (in Birrell 1971, p. 57).

[24] Rose 1994.

[25] Ibid.

[26] Rose 1994.

[27] Ginsburg 1989.

[28] Ibid.

rights and the development of the notion of *personality*.[29] The two regimes also reflect different approaches to copyright/authors' rights. In the United Kingdom (and other common-law countries), copyright balances the interest of the public and the author.[30] In contrast, the Dutch law is said to be based on the natural rights of authors.[31]

5.3.2 Romantic Authorship

Although authorship in the Statute of Anne was initially a facade to extend the power of booksellers, it slowly evolved into an individualistic notion of creativity. In effect, writers were no longer treated as craft people to be patronised by wealthy sponsors, such as printers. Instead, writers were now authors, who were deemed to hold the right to own the content of their writings. Their possession was not only limited to the physical object (i.e., the ink and paper) but also extended to the message they delivered through writing. Legal scholars often associated the development of authorship in the 18th century with the romantic movement in literature and art,[32] hence calling the glorification of authors' position in this period as 'romantic authorship'. Peter Jaszi suggests that such notion contains an 'implicit recognition of a hierarchy of artistic productions.'[33] In that hierarchy, he further explained, art is more valuable if it is sourced from one's imagination rather than their mere application.[34] This would later be related to the requirement for originality: that a work truly results from one's mind, without adapting or copying from any other previous works.

The notion of romantic authorship places the author at the centre of the process of creation but neglects the external influences that, in reality, may contributed to creating the work.[35] This leads to two important consequences in developing copyright. First, the author is isolated as an individual genius who creates works using all his ability and distinctiveness, that may distinguish it from the work of others. It results in what we know today as the requirement of personality: that the author should connected to his/her work. At a higher threshold, it even requires the author's personality to be reflected in the work. Second, the author is deemed as the original

[29] Grosheide mentions that 'by making reference to both the idea of the creator's personality as the source of his work and the genius concept particularly in the eighteenth century, it began to be promoted by philosophers that the creator not only had a property right in the physical products which carried his creations, but even in the ideas contained therein.' See Grosheide 2010.

[30] Bently et al. 2022, p. 36.

[31] In *A Tale of Two Copyrights*, Jane Ginsburg argues that various legislative texts in France recognized the importance of the public domain: that despite the importance of protecting one's rights for one's intellectual creation, it is also important that the work can be enjoyed by the public (in Ginsburg 1989, p. 1013).

[32] Jaszi 1991.

[33] Ibid.

[34] Ibid.

[35] Zemer 2007, p. 74.

thinker whose minds solely provides the inspiration to create works. This need for originality translates into a demand that a work made by an author without copying other works.

5.3.3 *Criticism of Romantic Authorship*

Postmodern scholarship on copyright often criticises romantic authorship. Peter Jaszi and Martha Woodmansee claim that authorial creations are collaborative. Woodmansee argues that this collaborative quality existed in the 18th century when the 'romantic author' as an ideal was at its height of influence.[36] Further, they argue that authorial creations have, over time, become increasingly collaborative and that this is due, in large part, to information and communication technologies that facilitate collaborative engagement and the circulation of works.[37] For example, the internet has enabled authors from around the world to create, add and modify works easily. This easy collaboration means authorial creations are ill-suited to the notion of romantic authorship that see the sole creator of works individually. It also troubles the 'personality requirement' since, as multiple authors are involved, whose personality is reflected in the works are hard to determine.

The notion of romantic authorship has also been criticised because it neglects the influence of a work's external environment. Lior Zemer argues that a work results from combining the things already available in the public domain with the author's subjectivity.[38] An author 'borrows' creativity from the commons and mixes it with his/her own input to create new works.[39] It emphasises that, though the work is 'original', it does not stand alone. It may be influenced by external factors: language, social culture, or even already-existing works. That is, in considering that a work stands alone without any external influence undermines the contribution of the public domain.

The arguments against romantic authorship have been revisited with contemporary networked forms of technology and certain creative practices. James Boyle shows how musical works are borrowed from previous works. For example, Kanye West's song "Gold Digger" (2005) samples Ray Charles Robinson's "I Got a Woman" (a 1955 number one RnB hit). Robinson's song was itself sampled from a 1904 gospel song, "Jesus Is All the World to Me" by Will Lamartine Thompson,[40] a song already in the public domain. It was thus legal. Nevertheless, West paid Robinson's heirs

---

[36] Woodmansee 1992.

[37] Ibid.

[38] Zemer 2007, p. 77.

[39] Such a borrowing and modifying practice can even be found in Western classical music prior to the 19th century (in Arewa 2013, p. 69).

[40] There was a suspicion that Robinson's "I Got a Woman" was sourced from "I've Got a Saviour" by the Harold Bailey Gospel Singers, but it was hard to trace both the origin of the song and who owns it, see Boyle 2008.

through licensing, thus justifying this sampling chain in the eyes of copyright law. Boyle, however, also points out cases where sampling practices present problematic for other creative practices and free speech. For example, in *Bridgeport Music, Inc v. Dimension Films.*

> The band NWA had used a tiny fragment (less than two seconds) consisting of three notes of a guitar solo from the George Clinton song "Get Off Your Ass and Jam." [...] A company called Bridgeport Music owned the sound recording copyright over the Clinton song. They sued. NWA's response was predictable—this was classic *de minimis* copying, which the law did not touch. One did not even have to get to the issue of fair use. (though this surely would be one)[41]

Although the court understood that recording music often works by borrowing from previous works, and that what "today's a sampler, tomorrow's a samplee", it refused to justify such creative practice under copyright law: "Get a license or do not sample" gives a strict sense that not even a snippet borrowed in recording music is allowed unless it is licensed. It does not consider the possibility of justifying the copying through the *de minimis* rule, which allows a small portion from previous works to be copied.

Another notable example of collaborative authorship was HBO's TV series, *Game of Thrones* (2011), which involved many creators. The show is distinctive in that its first five seasons were based on George R. R. Martin's novel, *A Song of Ice and Fire*, while the rest of the series was based on what David Benioff and D.B. Weiss, the show's executive producers, showrunners, and writers interpreted. The TV series ran for eight seasons from 2011 to 2019, during which the novelist, Benioff and Weiss collaborated. When the show was first aired, Martin had written five out of the seven books that he planned to publish. Starting from Season Five, Benioff and Weiss had to devise their own version of the story as Martin had not finished writing the final two books. Therefore, for Season Eight in 2019, because the books were not finished, Martin apprised Benioff and Weiss of the overview of how the story would have ended,[42] and let them decide the plots and story-lines for what was left.

Creative practices such as these strengthen the criticism of romantic authorship because any authorship is rarely, if ever, the work of a single person. Works are borrowed from previous works, either protected by copyright or in the public domain, and may be created by multiple authors. Unfortunately, since copyright in some jurisdictions remains heavily influenced by the notion of romantic author, it might not recognise the types of creative practices that were exemplified in the *Bridgeport* case.

---

[41] Boyle 2008.

[42] In an interview with the Guardian in 2011, George R.R. Martin describes himself as a 'gardener' type of writer who develops stories as he goes, meaning that while writing the stories he might not even know what the ending would be (in Flood 2011).

5.4 The Concept of Authorship in Indonesia and its Correlation to AI-generated Works

As mentioned earlier, Indonesian copyright law was initially drawn directly from Dutch law. After going through various amendments, the law has gradually come to better reflect Indonesia's political, economic, and social interests. Despite this, fundamental concepts such as the way that the author is seen, have not changed to any extent. While the notion of romantic author may be applied to books, poems, photographs and paintings, it is often difficult to apply to other types of creative works. As will be seen in the next chapter, this is the case with traditional cultural expressions, some large-scale databases, and AI-generated works.

Modern copyright law in Indonesia has gone through several amendments. Immediately post-Independence, copyright was seen as a foreign concept derived from the Dutch. As such, it was not enforced by the Indonesian government, nor were the country's inherited obligations under international intellectual property law agreements. As a result, Indonesia received international pressures to amend its law to comply with the standards of international copyright. The situation changed in 2002 when the laws were amended and copyright began to be gradually accepted and enforced in Indonesia.

Despite these changes, the way that the author is seen has remained the same. While the law allows either single authors or multiple authors to create works, it tends to appoint a single copyright owner of the work. The law also requires that the authors create a distinctive form of work having a personal characteristic.[43] The 1982, 1997 and 2002 Copyright Acts have respectively defined an author as 'a person or a group of persons from whose inspirations works are generated based on intellectual capabilities, imagination, dexterity, creativity, or expertise, fixated in a form and having a distinctive personal characteristic.' This implies that a person can be considered to be an author as long as he/she is a legal subject and is able to show creativity or expertise, and his/her personality is reflected in the work. The 2014 Copyright Act defines an author as 'a person or a group of persons, who either individually or jointly produce works that are distinct and personal.'[44] When compared to the earlier definitions, this article does not require creativity to be performed by an author. Nonetheless, the creativity element is required through the definition of a work.[45]

[43] Translated from the Indonesian: *'ciptaan yang bersifat khas dan pribadi.'*

[44] Article 1(2), *Law number 28 of 2014 on Copyright 2014 (Indonesia)* (2014 Copyright Act).

[45] In the 2014 Copyright Act, a work is defined as any creation in the field of science, art, and literature, produced based on inspiration, ability, thought, imagination, dexterity, creativity, or expertise, and manifested in a concrete form.

i) Works made by a person or a group of persons
The definition of an author in Indonesian law allows for a group of people to be recognised as co-authors. While Indonesian copyright law may acknowledge the possibility of multiple authorship the 2014 Copyright Act provides that even when a work is made by multiple authors, only one party is usually appointed as the author of the work. For example, Article 33 sub-article 1 of the 2014 Copyright Act provides that, "in the event that works comprise of several individual parts created by 2 (two) persons or more, the one that will be regarded as the author is the person leading and overseeing the completion of the entire works."[46]

This provision suggests that when two (or more) people are involved in creating a work that the author of the work is the person who leads and supervises the completion of the work.[47] This sub-article applies to compilations, where different authors contribute different parts that are compiled together to form the work. While at first blush this may appear to be relevant to AI-generated works, AI-generated works differ from compilations because they are not comprised of separate parts, even though multiple authors are involved in creating them. Further, Article 34 of the Indonesian Copyright Act provides that when 'a work is designed by a person and executed by another person under the direction and supervision of the person who designs, the author shall be the person designing the work.'[48] This article does not reflect the creation of AI-generated works because their end-result cannot be predicted nor designed. Programmers plan how the machine learning algorithm should function, and data trainers select training data relevant to its desired function, but do not design the AI-generated works and hence cannot be named as an author.

Even though the provisions in the Indonesian Copyright Act suggests that when a work is produced by multiple parties that assignment of a single author may be required; the Indonesian Copyright Register indicates differently. In the register, many works are registered under the name of more than one author.[49] There are two consequences of recording a work in the Indonesian Copyright Register. First, the authors are considered as copyright holders of the work. Where this is the case, any economic benefit arising from the use of the work will be distributed among the authors.[50] Second, an employer is named as the copyright holder of the work, while its creators are listed as authors. In this situation, economic benefits will be given to the employer as the copyright holder. The authors retain their moral rights, that is the right to be acknowledged as the author

---

[46] Article 33 (1), 2014 Copyright Act, above n. 44.

[47] A similar stipulation can also be found in *Article 6 of Law Number 6 of 1982 on Copyright* (1982 Copyright Act), *Law Number 12 of 1997 on the Revision of Law Number 6 of 1982 on Copyright* (1997 Copyright Act), and *Law Number 19 of 2002 on Copyright* (2002 Copyright Act) respectively.

[48] Article 34, 2014 Copyright Act, above n. 44.

[49] Works that often involve multiple authors in the Register of Copyright in Indonesia are software, learning modules, textbooks, journal articles, and choreographic works.

[50] Interview data.

of the work and the right to modify the work. In general, the first variation of the way interests is recorded in the copyright register may apply to AI-generated works, provided the programmers, data-trainers, and users are named as the authors of the work. If this was to occur, all of the named authors would be entitled to receive economic benefits arising from the AI-generated works being commercialised. This arrangement, however, would not permit generative AI to be a nominated author as it is not a legal subject.

ii) 'Works having a distinct form and personal characteristics'
The notion of romantic authorship is evident in the second requirement of authorship in Indonesian copyright law: namely, the requirement that the work must take a distinct form and contain personal characteristics. This requirement, which requires the author to be strongly related to their works, is similar to Dutch Copyright Act that requires an author's personality to be reflected in their work.[51] Personality is believed to be an important differentiating factor between a personal property and objects in the public domain,[52] because when a work reflects an author's personality, it is considered to be their property.[53] On the other hand, when a work does not reflect an author's personality, the work belongs in the public domain.

The connection between an author and his/her creation in Indonesia is signified by the personality test which requires that 1) the works result from the author's mind; and 2) the author has the knowledge about how such works are made. The scope of this provision can be seen in *Republic of Indonesia v Arifin,* where the defendant had infringed the author's copyright by selling counterfeit compact disks (CDs) of the author's songs.[54] The defendant failed to fulfil the personality test because the songs, sold in CDs, did not result from his mind, and he did not know how the songs were made.[55] In Indonesian jurisprudence, the personality test is often confused with the originality requirement. For example, in *Diesel Sp.A v Jemmy Wantono*, the respondent infringed the claimant's copyright by copying and publishing the 'Diesel-Only-The-Brave' picture. In this case, the personality test was used to assess whether the work was original and privately-owned, and whether it was a copy of other people's works.[56] Similar tests requiring originality are also present in other copyright-infringement cases.[57]

---

[51] Antons 2000, p. 60.

[52] Jened 2014, pp. 84–85.

[53] Ibid.

[54] *Republic of Indonesia v. Arifin No 35/Pid.Sus/2016/PN/Yyk.*

[55] Ibid.

[56] *Diesel Sp.A v Jemmy Wantono No 08/Pdt.Sus-Hak Cipta/2016/PN.Niaga.Jkt.Pst.*

[57] *Republic of Indonesia v Yudhi Dhani Wanto No 127/Pid.Sus/2016.PN.Smn, Republic of Indonesia v. Abdul Ajis No 128/Pid.Sus/2016/PN.Smn.*

The distinct and personal characteristics requirement builds upon the notion of romantic authorship which presumes that authors are individual geniuses. This view of the author is less relevant when multiple parties produce a work. There are a number of reasons why this requirement does not apply or is difficult to AI-generated works. First, AI-generated works have multiple contributors at different stages of creation, making it difficult if not impossible to identify the characteristics that are reflected in the work. Second, the involvement of generative AI in the creation of the works functions by executing commands, which has neither distinct nor personal characteristics that are able to be reflected in the resulting work.

The notion of the romantic author in the Indonesian copyright law necessitates that the author should be a person and that the author's personality should be reflected in the work. As discussed above, AI-generated works cannot meet those requirements because they are made by multiple authors, one of which is computer software. As a consequence, it would be challenging to identify whose personality is reflected in the AI-generated works. Because of this, it may be helpful to explore how Indonesia law has approached similar authorship problems in relation to traditional cultural expressions. This may offer important lessons for how the authorship of AI-generated works might be dealt with by Indonesian law.

5.5 Conclusion

Generative AI and its capacity of creating new works has strengthen the criticism towards the notion of the romantic author for at least two reasons. First, it necessitates a reflection of the authors' personality into the work, which becomes a challenge when a work is created by multiple authors. Such requirement reduces the possibility of accommodating AI-generated works into Indonesian copyright law, specifically because its creative process involves a number of contributors, in which one of them is a software that arguable does not have personality. Second, the notion of romantic author generally necessitates a limited number of authors. This requirement is often criticised for being unable to reflect creative practices is often hyper-authored. This is also the case in the production of AI-generated works which require contributions from a lot of people in multiple stages.

Since AI-generated works do not fit comfortably with Indonesian approaches to authorship, another approach is needed. The next two chapters explore alternative models for protecting AI-generated works with copyright-related rights. In Chap. 6, I explore the possibility of applying *sui generis* rights to protect works that do not meet copyright requirements, but still merit protection. In doing so, I look primarily at two existing *sui generis* rights, namely the *sui generis* right that protects traditional knowledge and traditional cultural expressions, which is proposed in Indonesia, and the *sui generis* database right, as put forward by the EU. In Chap. 7, I then explore the benefits and issues arising in relation to the use of neighbouring rights as a model to protect AI-generated works in Indonesia.

References

Antons C (2000) Intellectual Property Law in Indonesia. Kluwer Law International, The Netherlands

Arewa O B (2013) Making Music: Copyright Law and Creative Processes. In: Gray J, Johnson D (eds) A Companion to Media Authorship. Wiley-Blackwell, John Wiley & Sons Ltd, Chichester, pp. 69–87 https://doi.org/10.1002/9781118505526.ch4

Bently L et al. (2022) Intellectual property law, 6th edn. Oxford University Press, Oxford

Birrell A (1971) Seven lectures on the law and history of copyright in books. Rothman Reprints

Boyle J (2008) The Public Domain: Enclosing the Commons of the Mind. Yale University Press, London

Cronin B (2001) Hyperauthorship: A postmodern perversion or evidence of a structural shift in scholarly communication practices? Journal of the American Society for Information Science and Technology 52(7):558–569 https://doi.org/10.1002/asi.1097

Deazley R (2004) On the origin of the right to copy: Charting the movement of copyright law in eighteenth century Britain (1695–1775). Hart Publishing, Portland

Dent C (2014) Registers of artefacts of creation—from the late Medieval Period to the 19th Century. Laws 3(2):239–281 https://doi.org/10.3390/laws3020239

Feather J (1991) From rights in copies to copyright: The recognition of authors' rights in English law and practice in the sixteenth and seventeenth centuries. Cardozo Arts & Ent. LJ 10:455

Flood A (2011) Getting More from George RR Martin. The Guardian. https://www.theguardian.com/books/booksblog/2011/apr/14/more-george-r-r-martin

Ginsburg J C (1989) A Tale of Two Copyrights: Literary Property in Revolutionary France and America. Tulane Law Review 64(5):991–1031

Grosheide W (2010) Transition from guild regulation to modern copyright law–a view from the Low Countries. In: Bently L et al. (eds) Global Copyright. Edward Elgar Publishing, Cheltenham, pp. 79–102 https://doi.org/10.4337/9781849806428.00013

Huson G (2018) I, Copyright. Santa Clara High Technology Law Journal 35(2):54–78

Jaszi P (1991) Toward a theory of copyright: the metamorphoses of "authorship". Duke Law Journal 1991:455–502

Jened R (2014) Hukum Hak Cipta [Copyright Law]. Citra Aditya Bakti, Bandung

Lim D (2018) AI & IP: Innovation & Creativity in an Age of Accelerated Change. Akron Law Review 52:813–875

Melton J V H (2001) The Rise of the Public in Enlightenment Europe. Cambridge University Press, Cambridge https://doi.org/10.1017/CBO9780511819421

Nature Index (2018) Paper authorship goes hyper. https://www.nature.com/nature-index/news/paper-authorship-goes-hyper. Accessed 7 May 2022

Nogrady B (2023) Hyperauthorship: the publishing challenges for 'big team' science. Nature 615(7950): 175–177 https://doi.org/10.1038/d41586-023-00575-3

Rosati E (2018) The exception for text and data mining (TDM) in the proposed Directive on Copyright in the Digital Single Market. PE 604.942. European Parliament

Rose M (1994) The Author in Court: Pope v. Curll (1741). In: Woodmansee M, Jaszi P (eds) The Construction of Authorship: Textual Appropriation in Law and Literature. Duke University Press

Ross M B (1994) Authority and Authenticity: Scribbling Authors and the Genius of Print in Eighteenth-Century England. In: Woodmansee M, Jaszi P (eds) The Construction of Authorship: Textual Appropriation in Law and Literature. Duke University Press

Samuelson P (1986) Allocating Ownership Rights in Computer-Generated Works. University of Pittsburgh Law Review 47:1185–1228

Woodmansee M (1992) On the author effect: Recovering collectivity. Case Legal Studies Research Paper No. 1992, Cardozo Arts & Entertainment L.J. 10:279–292

Zemer L (2007) The Idea of Authorship in Copyright. Ashgate Publishing Ltd., Hampshire, England

Chapter 6
Sui Generis Protection for AI-generated Works

Contents

Abstract *Sui generis* rights are designed to protect subject matters that cannot meet traditional intellectual property requirements, but that for some reasons still require protection. This is especially relevant for AI-generated works. Therefore, this chapter explores existing *sui generis* rights as potential frameworks for protecting AI-generated works. First, it evaluates *sui generis* rights for the protection of traditional cultural expressions in Indonesia and concludes that this model is unsuitable for AI-generated works because it emphasises community ownership and is often implemented locally. Second, it assesses *sui generis* database rights in the European Union and finds that both database and AI-generated works protection aim to protect technological investment rather than authorship. However, the *sui generis* database rights are only applicable within the EU, while generative AI necessitates globally-accepted regulations because its production, distribution, and consumption process often transcends national boundaries. Therefore, a comprehensive international framework is essential for the effective protection of AI-generated works.

L. Andrini, *Protecting Artificial Intelligence-generated Works in Indonesia*, Information Technology and Law Series 41, https://doi.org/10.1007/978-94-6265-703-8_6

Keywords *Sui generis* right · Database right · *Sui generis* rights for traditional cultural expressions · WIPO · TRIPs · Text and data mining · Fair use · Regulatory exceptions

6.1 Introduction

Sui generis intellectual property regimes provide protection for creations that do not fit into the typical intellectual property rights regime, but still merit protection.[1] Over time there have been several examples of successful *sui generis* protection including plant breeders' rights, farmers' rights, and semiconductor chip protection.

In this chapter I look at two different *sui generis* regimes that have the potential to act as models for the protection of AI-generated works. The first are the laws which have been proposed in Indonesia to protect traditional cultural expression. The second is the European Union (EU)'s *sui generis* database right. These *sui generis* rights have been selected as both objects of protection are of interest to multiple and varied stakeholders. In this way these objects of protection are similar to AI-generated works which also involve numerous stakeholders and give rise to non-traditional models of authorship that challenge copyright requirements. Additionally, the planned protection for traditional cultural expression has been developed within Indonesian context and provides a jurisdictional fit, whereas the database right has been developed to address issues relating to similar technological subject matter.

In general, *sui generis* rights are promising because they address specific concerns and challenges that are not readily answered by the typical intellectual property mechanisms. Specifically, this chapter explore whether the Indonesian *sui generis* right for traditional cultural expressions, which aspires to protect community interests in intangible cultural heritage, and the EU database right, which protects the varied investments necessary to create databases, can be productive comparators for conceptualizing appropriate protections for AI-generated works.[2] Even though a *sui generis* right can provide tailored legal protection for non-traditional objects, they have some drawbacks. First, the application of a *sui generis* right tends to only apply within the jurisdictional reach of the nation-state within which it is enacted. As such, *sui generis* rights lack international uniformity—a desirable feature vis-à-vis regulatory frameworks for new and emerging technologies. Different jurisdictions oversee different objects of protection and diverse ways of protecting them. Consequently, harmonising *sui generis* protection across different jurisdictions becomes challenging. This can prove challenging within the context of new and emerging technologies which are both developed by and deployed across numerous jurisdictions. Second, *sui generis* rights have the potential to overlap with existing intellectual

[1] Maidanyk 2021, p. 151.

[2] Hugenholtz 2016, p. 221.

property rights and create legal uncertainties. The EU database right, for example, overlaps with copyright law and confuses database producers and users.[3]

In the first section of this chapter, I discuss the lessons that we can draw for AI-generated works based upon the Indonesian efforts to provide a *sui generis* model of protection to traditional cultural expressions. Specifically, I look at how Indonesian copyright law plans to deal with the collective authorship of traditional cultural expressions, which in many ways are socially conceptualised as hyper-authored creations embodying communal interests and drawing from communal resources produced by generations past and present. In this sense, providing copyright protection to individual authors of specific expressions of intangible cultural heritage is incompatible with Indonesian social understandings of the creative process required to produce and making meaningful use of these traditional works. Consequently, the Indonesian government proposes to use *sui generis* rights to protect traditional works that reflects this social understanding. I explore the potential for this model, which has been developed within and for the Indonesian context, to meet domestic social values for works involving numerous contributors, such as AI-generated works.

The second section of this chapter focuses on database rights in the EU as regulated in the Directive 96/9/EC on the Legal Protection of Databases (i.e., a Database Directive) as a potential model law to protect AI generated works. Even though the directive does not apply to Indonesia, there are two reasons why the EU *sui generis* database right makes an idea model of protection. First, the EU is the first jurisdiction to introduce a legal framework to protect databases through the *sui generis* right. Other countries who wish to establish the *sui generis* right for database always refer to the EU database directive. Second, this directive may indirectly affect the interests of database creators in Indonesia, as its scope of protection is limited to the nationals of member states.

Regarding the potential of this database right to restrict access to training data, this chapter addresses questions about text and data mining, a necessary step to train generative AI's algorithm used to create AI-generated works. While more training data is necessary to increase the accuracy of AI algorithms used to create AI-generated works, data scientists often find that acquiring training data is difficult because these works are protected by copyright. Similar problems arise if the data are owned by the citizen of, and/or located in, the territory of member states, because they are protected by a database right. To create a more supportive setting for developing AI-generated works, a more relaxed rule should be established to protect copyright in databases. To respond to such need, some jurisdictions have introduced measures to allow text and data mining. The United States, for example, justifies text and data mining by a fair use doctrine, while the EU has introduced limited exceptions that allow text and data mining for the purpose of training AI algorithms.

---

[3] Vollmer 2018.

6.2 *Sui Generis* Right for Traditional Cultural Expressions and AI-generated Works

Article 1 of WIPO's Draft on the Protection of Traditional Cultural Expressions defines traditional cultural expressions as:

> any forms, in which traditional culture practices and knowledge are expressed, [appear or are manifested] [the result of intellectual activity, experiences, or insights] by indigenous [peoples], local communities and/or [other beneficiaries] in or from a traditional context, and may be dynamic and evolving and comprise verbal forms, musical forms, expressions by movement, tangible or intangible forms of expression, or combinations thereof.[4]

One notable aspect about this definition is that it presupposes that traditional cultural expressions result from communal effort and that they are created by the community for its greater benefit. This is the case in Indonesia where traditional cultural expressions are not created for financial reasons so much as to express communal identity and to complement certain rituals. Agus Sardjono offers the example of a shamanic healer, a person believed to have power to cure sick people[5] who, because they are not motivated to enrich themselves,[6] are usually willing to share recipes for their traditional medicines without being worried that it may be copied by others.

Batik patterns[7] are commonly used in Indonesia to express communal identity. Historically, traditional batik patterns were only created by family members of a particular kingdom. Over time this has changed so that batik can now be created by any batik-maker, rather than being restricted to certain people in local kingdoms. Traditional dances in Indonesia have also been modified over time. *Pendet* dance from Bali, for example, used to be considered a sacred dance that could only be performed at religious rituals.[8] This has also changed over time. For example, *pendet* dances are now often performed to welcome tourists coming to Bali.[9] In Central Java, Bedhaya and Srimpi are well-known dances which represent an ideal figure of femininity in the Javanese culture.[10] While these dances were initially limited, they now take many forms as these expressions have been developed and modified over time.[11]

---

[4] Article 1, *Draft Articles of the Protection of Traditional Cultural Expressions, 19 June 2019, WIPO/GRTKF/IC/40/5.*

[5] Sardjono 2004, p. 147.

[6] Ibid.

[7] Batik is a traditional technique of applying wax onto a piece of fabric, and immersing the fabric into a dye bath. The process is done several times to produce a particular batik pattern.

[8] Astini and Utina 2007, pp. 170–171.

[9] Ibid.

[10] Morrison 1978.

[11] Ibid. p. 189. One variation of the Bedhaya dances called *Bedhaya Semang* could only be taught, practiced, and performed inside a palace because of its sacred nature. Unfortunately, these restrictions ultimately led to the extinction of the dance. Miriam J Morrison explained that there was an effort to revive the *Bedhaya Semang* dance in 1971, but the result was not conclusive. A later report

Originally, most traditional cultural expressions in Indonesia had a sacred or religious value. This is the key reason why authorship was limited to certain groups of people, such as religious leaders, authorities, or noble families[12] who have power to connect with the divine.[13] Over time, this reverence of traditional works has been transformed for entertainment purposes so that that lay people are now able to copy and modify the 'traditional' works. Such a practice does not accord with modern copyright law, as copying and modifying an existing work without its original author's authorisation may be considered to infringe copyright.

At least two consequences arising from the copying and modification of Indonesia's tradition. The first, is that this helps to disseminate and preserve traditional cultural expressions. As mentioned earlier, when the sacred value of a dance is preserved, the dance can only be performed in limited circumstances thus threatening its survival. In contrast, by allowing a dance to be performed for non-sacred purposes (such as entertainment) it could be argued that this helps to preserve the dance (albeit in a modified form).

Secondly, copying and modifying traditional cultural expression distorts the original version of the expression. This is especially true for unrecorded expressions whose existence predates digital recording technology. Since tracing the original version of the expressions is difficult, the current generation is only left with guidelines for performing the expressions but the freedom to create new variations of them. In this sense, the practices of copying and modifying traditional cultural expressions is at odds with the concept of originality in the modern copyright law, which requires that the work be the product of the author's mind and that it should not be copied from anywhere else.[14] However, that is not the case with traditional cultural expressions in Indonesia, which are created through copying and modifying earlier versions.

Two of the lessons we can draw from the way that traditional cultural expressions are made and preserved is that 1) the authorship of traditional works is not exclusive, and 2) its creation involves both copying and modifying, repeated from time to time, to vary expressions. These characteristics correspond to AI-generated works. First, authorship is not exclusive and involves multiple parties contributing to different resources that are all necessary for creating the work. One (or more) of these parties are non-sentient beings: traditional works have authors who may have passed away centuries ago, while AI-generated works have machine learned algorithms as non-human subjects. Second, generative AI learns established patterns from the learning data to generate new patterns within AI-generated works. This differs from copying and modifying traditional works as the former creates a new object, while the latter modifies the pre-existing creation.

---

by Indonesia's Department of Communication in 1999 shows that the *Bedhaya Semang* dance has become extinct, see Republik Indonesia 1999, p. 139.

[12] Nonetheless, there are also instances where the authors are unknown because the works had already existed for a long time and there were no official records to show who created the work in the first place.

[13] Hartley 2013.

[14] Wong and Fernandini 2010, p. 185.

Traditional cultural expressions, which entail a different creative process from that of conventional literary and artistic works, do not meet the requirement of modern copyright law especially regarding authorship and originality. Traditional cultural expressions cannot fulfil the originality requirement because their creative process involves modifying and copying. Furthermore, they cannot fulfil the personality requirement as the creation involves multiple authors throughout different generations, and more often than not, the original authors are hard to identify. However, protecting these expressions is necessary to safeguard against illegitimate claims by third parties and to preserve communal and/or national identities. Providing copyright protections to individual authors of specific expressions of intangible cultural heritage is incompatible with Indonesian social understandings of the creative process required to produce and making meaningful use of these traditional works.

With a gradual realisation that copyright is not suitable to protect traditional cultural expression in Indonesia, there has growing push for the development of *sui generis* rights to protect traditional works. This came to head in 2008 when the *Traditional Knowledge and Traditional Cultural Expressions (TKTCE) Bill* was released. While the Bill has not progressed to law, in so far as it attempts to protect non-traditional forms of authorship, it has the potential to act as a model when thinking about how to protect multi-authored AI-generated works.

6.2.1 **Sui Generis** ***Protection for Traditional Cultural Expressions***

Current Indonesian copyright law gives ownership over traditional cultural expressions to the nation-State for an indefinite time.[15] It also obligates the nation-State to maintain, preserve. and keep an inventory of traditional cultural expressions.[16] These provisions offer a useful way of protecting traditional cultural expressions against ownership claims by foreign countries because there have previously been several overlapping claims regarding traditional cultural expressions between Indonesia and Malaysia, among others concerning *batik,* the *Rasa Sayange* song, and *pendet* dance.[17]

The protection of traditional cultural expressions in Indonesian copyright law is, unfortunately, less than ideal, particularly in terms of cultural preservation by the specific community to which the practice is tied. As previously discussed, most traditional cultural expressions are practiced, performed, transmitted, and informally regulated within a particular community according to social norms and values. This means that the community, rather than the nation-state, is supposed to play a central

---

[15] Article 38 and 60(1), *Law number 28 of 2014 on Copyright 2014 (Indonesia)* (2014 Copyright Act).

[16] Ibid.

[17] Chong 2012, pp. 2–4.

role in safeguarding and preserving the traditional cultural expressions. This is particularly problematic in a highly culturally heterogenous country such as Indonesia, which is home to more than 1300 ethnic groups speaking more than 700 distinct languages—many of whom have uneasy relationships with the nation-state.[18] Given such diversity, many communities may not feel their social values and norms are best represented by the nation-state. This concern is addressed in the Draft of the *Traditional Knowledge and Traditional Cultural Expressions (TKTCE) Bill* of 2008. The Bill acknowledges the role of communities in safeguarding traditional cultural expressions,[19] and better reflects how traditional cultural expressions are used within communities.

The Traditional Knowledge and Traditional Cultural Expressions Bill differs from the Indonesian Copyright Act in a number of ways. First, the Bill acknowledges communal ownership over traditional knowledge and traditional cultural expressions while copyright law encourages individual ownership. Under the bill, traditional knowledge and traditional cultural expressions is owned and maintained by a custodian community.[20] In this role, the community has authority to consent to other parties (users) if they wish to use its traditional knowledge and traditional cultural expressions.[21] The community is also entitled to share in benefits arising from using their traditional knowledge and traditional cultural expressions. In contrast, copyright law, which emphasises individual ownership of a work, grants ownership of traditional knowledge and traditional cultural expressions to Indonesia as a nation-State. Therefore, any use of traditional knowledge and traditional cultural expressions by foreign parties requires the nation-State's permission through the Ministry of Justice and Human Rights. Second, the Traditional Knowledge and Traditional Cultural Expressions Bill grants protection without requiring the 'standard' prerequisites of copyright protection, namely fixation, authorship and creativity. These requirements are seen to be incompatible with traditional knowledge and traditional cultural expressions whose creation involves copying and modification by multiple authors across different generations.

6.2.2 Using **Sui Generis** *Traditional Cultural Expressions Protection as a Model for AI-generated Works*

Globally, there has been an accelerating discussion critiquing the use of intellectual property rights to manage traditional cultural expressions, as well as an increasing demand for some form of cultural property protections for these socially important

[18] Ananta et al. 2015.

[19] Kariodimedjo 2019.

[20] The custodian community is understood to be the holder of rights and the recipient of benefits from the management of traditional knowledge/traditional cultural expressions including local, *adat,* and traditional communities (in ibid. p. 347).

[21] Ibid. pp. 350–355.

works. This is reflected in the work of scholars, activists, and communities and its recognition is reflected in the establishment of programming efforts at the international governmental level, such as the World Intellectual Property Organization. Interest in this space is growing rapidly due to the recognition that traditional cultural expressions not only serve as works of literature or arts, but that they are also part of the social identity of specific communities and their creation and circulation is an important aspect of social cohesion and survival. Thus, the protection of traditional cultural works is important.[22]

The Indonesian government's initiative in drafting the Traditional Knowledge and Traditional Cultural Expressions Bill to deal with the authorship issues associated with traditional knowledge and traditional cultural expressions opens up the possibility of using a similar approach to deal with AI-generated works: which destabilises copyright's prerequisite of authorship and creativity. In this sense, the *sui generis* right for traditional cultural expressions provides an alternative model to protect AI-generated works: not least because they are created by multiple authors. In the Traditional Knowledge and Traditional Cultural Expressions Bill, the traditional cultural expression is owned by the custodian, that is the community or traditional society who maintains or develops traditional knowledge and traditional cultural expressions traditionally and communally.[23]

While this approach might be feasible to protect traditional cultural expressions owned by a particular community or traditional society, there are two reasons why this approach will not work to protect AI-generated works. First, the contributors of AI-generated works often come from different organisations. Giving ownership of AI-generated works to the custodian would not be practical because it would mean that a decision would need to be made about whether the programmers, data trainers, or users should be the owner of copyright. This scheme also defies the essence of communal authorship as envisaged by the *sui generis* right for traditional cultural expressions. Alternatively, another organisation would need to be established that could act as custodian of AI-generated works. However, this is not practical because generative AI software can produce a massive amount of AI-generated works in a

[22] Traditional cultural expressions are not only discussed in the middle-income countries. It also becomes problematic in countries such as Australia. In *Bulun Bulun & Anor v R & T Textiles Pty Ltd.*, Mr. Bulun Bulun filed a lawsuit for copyright infringement because his painting of *Magpie Geese and Waterlilies at the Waterhole* was printed and reproduced on textile without his approval. The painting itself was made in accordance with the laws and traditions of *Ganalbingu* people, a native Australian group, whose elders had given Bulun Bulun permission to do so. Nonetheless the lawsuit involved two claimants: first, Mr. Bulun Bulun who sought copyright over the painting. Second, Mr George M who represented the *Ganalbingu* people in claiming they were the equitable owners of copyright subsisting in the painting. Regarding the copyright claim regarding traditional cultural expressions, Justice Von Doussa observed that communal ownership over intellectual property is not acknowledged in Australia. However, there was a fiduciary relationship between Mr. Bulun Bulun and the *Ganalbingu* people that meant Mr. Bulun Bulun was obligated to protect the traditional expressions of the community (in *John Bulun Bulun & M v. R & T Textiles Pty Ltd (1998)* (John Bulun Bulun & M v. R & T Textiles Pty Ltd)).

[23] Article 1 (5), Indonesia's Traditional Knowledge and Traditional Cultural Expressions Bill.

relatively short time. Establishing a custodian for each AI-generated work would not be successful as it would increase the cost and time of producing such works.

Another reason why the approach used in relation to traditional cultural expressions may not be suitable to protect AI-generated works is because they follow different purposes. While the Traditional Knowledge and Traditional Cultural Expressions Bill is designed to protect communal creations against private interests, any law that protects AI-generated works, especially in Indonesian, needs to safeguard the investment of private parties involved in its creation while also guaranteeing public access to knowledge. From this perspective, some provisions in the Traditional Knowledge and Traditional Cultural Expressions Bill do not work for AI-generated works. For example, Article 4, which suggests that traditional knowledge and traditional cultural expressions will be protected as long as it continues to be maintained by its custodians, would apply to AI-generated works. Instead of being protected for a very long time, AI-generated works should be protected for a short time to balance the public and private interests.

6.3 Database Rights and AI-generated Works

The second area of law that potentially operates as a model for how we might protect AI-generated works is the EU's *sui generis* database right. It is important to note that the database right operates like a double-edged sword in relation to AI-generated works. On the one hand, it potentially acts as a model for protecting AI-generated works that do not fit into the current copyright regime. On the other hand, the database right also creates a potential barrier to using data that are essential for training the algorithms embedded in generative AI systems.

6.3.1 The First Edge of the Sword: The Database Right as a Model for Protecting AI-generated Works

In general, databases can attract copyright protection as a compilation so long as the underlying organisational logic requires some creative labour (e.g., is not subject to a natural ordering, such as alphabetical or numerical). However, the level of protection is considered very thin and is located in the organisational logic. Because the originality of many data compilations is doubtful or attract such thin protection, some jurisdictions, such as the EU, have introduced extra protection for databases by developing *sui generis* right. Under such laws, databases are accorded two tiers of protection, namely copyright and *sui generis* protection.[24] The former protects the selection and/or arrangement of the database in that they are considered to be an author's intellectual creation and thus subject to copyright. The *sui generis* rights

[24] Gupta 2017, p. 1.

protect the content of databases even though this content is not deemed to comprise intellectual creations and thus may require substantial investment. The EU introduced the *sui generis* database right to incentivise investment. Copyright and database rights may co-exist in the same database as long as the relevant requirements are satisfied. For copyright protection, this means that the requirements for fixation, authorship, and originality are met. In contrast, the database right only requires that a substantial investment has been made in 'obtaining, verification, and/or re-utilization of the whole, or of a substantial part, evaluated qualitatively and/or quantitatively, of the contents of that database.'[25]

6.3.2 Copyright Protection of Databases

One of the common features of international and national copyright law is that copyright only protects the arrangement and not the content of databases. As Article 5 of the WIPO Copyright Treaty provides:

> Compilations of data or other material, in any form, which by reason of the selection or arrangement of their contents constitute intellectual creations, are protected as such. This protection does not extend to the data or the material itself and is without prejudice to any copyright subsisting in the data or material contained in the compilation.[26]

A similar provision is found in the EU Database Directive, where a database is defined as a 'collection of independent works, data, or other materials arranged in a systematic or methodical way and individually accessible by electronic or other means.'[27] A similar provision also exists in Indonesian copyright law where selecting or arranging data in databases is considered intellectual work worthy of copyright protection.[28] In contrast, the main reason why copyright law does not protect the content of databases is because it does not meet the 'originality' criterion.[29] As a result, copyright protection is limited to selecting or arranging the data in a database.

At first glance, the creation of AI-generated works may be mistakenly understood as being similar to the creation of databases. Arguably, however, the way that these two technological objects are created differs significantly. First, because databases consist of numerous pre-existing data that are arranged according to specific rules, the information remains the same when it is integrated into a database. In contrast, creating AI-generated works relies on training data that are used only to train the AI algorithm in understanding and creating a certain pattern that is repeated in the resulting creation. Even though an AI-generated work may contain aspects of the

---

[25] Article 7, *Directive 96/9/EC of the European Parliament and of the Council on the Legal Protection of Databases, European Communities (entered into force 11 March 1996)* (Database Directive).

[26] Article 5, *WIPO Copyright Treaty* (WIPO Copyright Treaty).

[27] Article 1(2), Database Directive, above n. 25.

[28] Elucidation of Article 40(1)(n), 2014 Copyright Act, above n. 15.

[29] 'Copyright in databases' in Bainbridge 2019.

training data, it is a whole new object that differs from the training data. Second, because databases can be treated as compilations, they are subject to copyright protection, while AI-generated works, not being compilations, require a different legal framework to accommodate their idiosyncrasies.

6.3.2.1 *Sui Generis* Protection of Databases

Underlying the EU database right is the idea that as the content of databases often result from substantial investment, they need to be protected.[30] This content is not subject to copyright protection because it lacks an author's intellectual creation.[31] Therefore, to safeguard the substantial investment in a database's creation, in 1996 the EU introduced the *sui generis* database right.[32] To date, Indonesia has not adopted anything like the database right, leaving databases to be protected by copyright. Irrespective of how databases are selected and/or arranged, their content remains unprotected.

i) The scope of the Database Right

The EU database right protects the owner of the database from its unauthorised extraction and/or reuse, but also allows lawful users to extract and/or use insubstantial parts of the database.[33] The protection lasts for 15 years from the January 1 of the following year after the database is completed or made public.[34] If is contents change substantially (with substantial new investment), the revised database will receive a new term of protection.[35]

ii) The 'substantial investment' requirement

To apply, the EU database right only requires that there be a substantial investment in the creation of the database. Unlike copyright, it does not require authorship, creativity or originality. So long as the creation of the database involves a substantial investment, either quantitatively or qualitatively in the process of collecting, verifying, and presenting these three requirements, it can be protected by the database right.[36] This type of protection may apply to AI-generated works because creating them according to software objectives, the learning process, and producing AI-generated works also requires investment.

As the Database Directive does not explain what is meant by a 'substantial investment', courts in EU member states must interpret this phrase on a case-by-case basis.[37] To do this, a court must decide whether there has been a quantitative and qualitative investment in the collecting, verifying and presenting the

---

[30] Bensinger 1999, pp. 27 and 154 in Beunen 2007, p. 68.

[31] 'Copyright in databases' in Bainbridge 2019.

[32] Recitals 15 and 58, Database Directive, above n. 25.

[33] Article 8(2), ibid.

[34] Article 10, ibid.

[35] Article 10 (3), ibid.

[36] Derclaye 2005, p. 5.

[37] Ibid.

database. While the quantitative requirement can be shown through any financial investment made,[38] the qualitative investment is typically demonstrated through the skills and expertise required to create the database.[39]

Research by Estelle Derclaye suggests that the substantiality of investment has a relatively low threshold.[40] As long as the investment results in a database and can be made by anyone, it will be considered as a substantial investment.[41] While, in some situations, the database right has been granted where there have been substantial investments, in other cases, the database right has been recognised where only a couple hundred euros have been invested.[42]

Like the creation of databases, the process of creating AI-generated works can also involve a wide variation in terms of quantity and quality of investment. A large investment, both in terms of labour and finance, is generally needed when the learning process uses a large amount of data. In this situation, data scientists may invest a lot of time to collect, verify, and prepare the data required to train the generative AI system. In other situations, they may need to create learning data on their own. This usually occurs when the existing data needed to train the algorithm is protected by copyright.[43]

Users of generative AI software also invest in several other ways. Many AI-generated works require additional human involvement in order to finalise the product. This is readily exemplified in the case discussed at the start of this chapter. In this scenario the software user, the fashion designer, needed to transpose the *Rinna* scarf pattern onto a textile to convert it into a wearable garment that is ready for sale. In this scenario, the software user's qualitative investment may take the form of selecting the most suitable scarf design and applying the design to a tangible medium, while their quantitative investment may take the form of running the fashion company and paying the employees. In other instances, users may not be required to do anything after the generative AI system produces the AI-generated works. However, the software user may still be required to pay a certain amount of money to the provider to access and use the generative AI system.[44] Given the low threshold of substantial investment in creating a database, if a database-style right was applied, users of generative AI requiring a low threshold for operation may possibly qualify for protection. This would be conditional on software user showing that they contributed in some

[38] Hugenholtz 2001, pp. 2–3.

[39] Beunen 2007, p. 104.

[40] Derclaye 2005, p. 9.

[41] Hugenholtz 2016.

[42] In France, for example, *Sonacotra v. Syndicat Sud Sonacotra* is concerned with whether a database of 1,650 employees' email addresses is subject to a *sui generis* database right. It was held that the said database is protected by the database right because Sonacotra had put both financial and human investment into the update and maintenance of such a list (Derclaye 2005).

[43] Some jurisdictions like the EU and Singapore have introduced an exception to copyright protection for text and data mining. In such an exception, using pre-existing data to train algorithms for educational purposes would not be considered a copyright infringement.

[44] Some web-based generative AI providers usually impose subscription fees on their users.

manner to the resulting work (or the means of generating the AI-generated work).

iii) International application of Database Rights

In 1996 the EU was the first jurisdiction to introduce the *sui generis* database right through its Directive 96/9/EC. The scope of protection of this Directive is limited to EU member states and incorporated companies that have registered offices in a member state.[45] The Council of the EU has authority to extend such database protection to nationals or residents of non-member states within special agreements[46] required as a basis of reciprocity between the EU and non-member states to provide database protections. In other words, the *sui generis* database right would only accord with databases made by the nationals of non-EU member states if they have agreed to give similar protection to databases made by the nationals of member states.

Indonesia, as a non-member state of the EU, does not fall under the scope of the database right. Indonesia also does not have a special agreement with the EU to protect database by way of the *sui generis* right. However, this means that the Directive can impact upon non-member states, such as Indonesia. In my view, the EU database right creates a different treatment between databases generated in member states and non-member states. For example, when a national of a member state uses a database sourced from Indonesia, it is only protected by copyright, not the *sui-generis* database right. As discriminatory as it may sound, this is justified as the database right is not subject to the Trade Related Aspects of Intellectual Property (TRIPs) agreement and its principle of national treatment.

National treatment is a general principle acknowledged by members of the World Trade Organization to provide nationals of other member states a "no-less-favourable" treatment to the protection given its own nationals.[47] The national treatment principle is also included in other World Trade Organization agreements, notably the TRIPs agreement. It safeguards intellectual property, such as copyright, trademarks, geographical indications, industrial designs, patents, integrated circuits and trade secrets. Unfortunately, *sui generis* rights, as modified rights, do not fall under the scope of TRIPs agreement (except in the case of plant innovations). As a result, any country can introduce a novel right in its national jurisdiction without having to adhere to the TRIPS agreement.[48]

The EU database right, which was introduced to protect databases, focuses more on the protection of investment in the process of producing works, rather than the works themselves.[49] The database right does not require that there be intellectual efforts in making databases. The only requirement is that there be substantial investment in selecting, classifying and presenting the data. This

---

[45] Article 11, Database Directive, above n. 25.

[46] Hugenholtz 2016, p. 220.

[47] Articles 1 and 2, *Agreement on Trade-Related Aspects of Intellectual Property Rights, opened for signature 15 April 1994 (entered into force 1 January 1995)* (TRIPs Agreement).

[48] Westkamp 2003, pp. 832–835.

[49] Hugenholtz 2016, p. 217.

makes it more difficult for the *sui generis* database right to be a part of the TRIPs agreement, whose original purpose was to establish a standard of protecting intellectual properties.[50]

Since national treatment does not apply, databases from non-EU member states are only protected by the database right if the originating countries grant the database right to nationals of member states in their jurisdiction. While the reciprocity requirement is understandable and in line with the purpose of protecting database owners in the EU from unauthorised extractions, the exclusivity is impractical. In this era where information, data and databases are stored in the cloud, and can be accessed, edited and exchanged online by anyone from anywhere in the world, exclusivity based on geographical limitation is redundant.

This book contends that copyright law should and needs to reflect the reality that most new and emerging technologies are increasingly created by teams and are used by parties in numerous different jurisdictions. This means that any copyright or similar protections afforded to AI generated systems, related training databases, and AI-generated works should be able to reach beyond national borders if these regulatory frameworks are to be of any practical use. As such, standardised international protection for database rights must be established. As Mark Davison argues, the database right is actually a form of copyright by another name. Davison supports his arguments by comparing the requirement for the database right according to copyright's *sweat-of-the-brow* theory.[51] Further, he asserts that the owner of copyright in a database also possesses the *sui generis* database right, with similar rights and exceptions.[52] For those similarities, he argues that the database right qualifies as a type of intellectual property under the TRIPs agreement and, as such, the principle of national treatment should apply.

6.3.2.2 Applying the Database Right to AI-generated Works

Databases and AI-generated works are similar because their creation requires investment. However, they differ in how they present their sources of data. As explained earlier, databases are sourced from pre-existing data that can still be identified within the database. In contrast, AI-generated works are produced by generative AI, whose algorithm has been trained using training data. In other words, AI-generated works are wholly new creations that cannot be connected to specific training data, even though those data are used to train generative AI. In this next section, I assess whether the EU database right can be used as a model law to protect AI-generated works.

i) *Who should own the sui generis right in AI-generated works?*

---

[50] Preambule, TRIPs Agreement, above n. 47.

[51] According to 'sweat of the brow', someone can be considered the author of the work as long as he/she can demonstrate that he/she has expended a significant effort on creating the work (in Davison 1998).

[52] Ibid.

The EU database right protects the maker of the database against unauthorised extractions. Such protection is given to honour the investment made by the creator of databases. In copyright terms, the database right only protects economic interests and does not extend to the moral rights of contributors. Following this logic, the owner of a database-style right for AI-generated works should be those who invested their time, skill, and money in the AI-generated works.

In this regard, two things need to be considered: First, the investment must impact directly on the creation of AI-generated works. This requirement needs to be highlighted because the making of AI-generated works involves multiple stages, namely determining the objective, data training, and creating the final product.[53] Each stage requires investments from different contributors: in the first and second stages this usually results in an algorithm that is embedded in software, which are protected by software copyright.[54] On the other hand, the investment made in the third stage (i.e., in creating AI-generated works) is not protected by copyright or any other proprietary right. Because the investment made by users helps to determine whether a work is produced and when this happens that the work is circulated to the public, it does not seem fair that their investments are not recognised.[55]

In this context, there is no good reason why a database style right should not be given to users to protect their investments in creating AI-generated works—protection that would stimulate the advance of machine learning. It would also ensure that a legal framework is prepared to safeguard the investments of users, or anyone who takes part in creating AI-generated works. Such a scheme would encourage investment in generative AI and thus boost the progress of science in AI and machine learning.

If this was adopted, there should not be a requirement that substantial investment be occurred as a pre-condition of protection since the creation of AI-generated works does not require substantial investment. Instead, to avoid doubt, it would be more fitting if a requirement for 'minimal investment' was adopted though it does not accord with how the EU has construed 'substantial investment'.[56] Eliminating the requirement of substantial investment for AI-generated works would prevent disputes among software programmers, data trainers and users about who had invested the most and thus deserves to be the owner of the *sui generis* right for AI-generated works. If the decision about who the owner

[53] Lehr and Ohm 2017, p. 655.

[54] Robert Yu explains that rewarding the software programmers would result in over-rewards and invites copyright stockpiling. This would later on result in copyright infringement litigation that would not be beneficial to the public (in Yu 2017, p. 1261).

[55] Ibid.

[56] Sandra Gosnell mentions that "it seems plausible that most kinds of investment in any database context will be substantial [...] thus, even the most mundane compilations, such as Greater Union's list of cinema screening times, will be protected since there has been some input of time, money, and effort through technical, financial, or human means." In Gosnell 2003, p. 660.

is, is determined according to who invested most, then the ownership of AI-generated works would almost always go to programmers or data trainers. This would create a barrier for those interested in generative AI software to produce works because they would receive nothing from it. A lack of interest by software users in using generative AI and contributing to the creation of AI-generated works, may have knock-on effects so that software engineers and data scientists might not be adequately supported to continue developing these systems.

ii) Duration of Protection

Since the primary purpose of a database style right for AI-generated works right would be to protect investments, the works should receive protection for long enough to provide an equitable return-on-investment.[57] This is something that would need to be determined on the basis of empirical research (which is beyond the scope of this book).

iii) *International application of a sui generis rights for AI-generated works*

I have previously suggested that extending the EU database right to people of non-member states is impractical given that creating databases is rarely restricted to single jurisdictions. Similarly, making AI-generated works cannot be limited to a single country. For example, a generative AI system developed by a software company in Indonesia may use training data from China. The software may then be used by others in many countries, such as the United Kingdom, India, Italy, Japan and South Korea to create AI-generated works. The absence of national treatment in such a scenario will create an unfair condition for users who can rely only on the protection provided by their national jurisdictions. When their works cross national boundaries, that the works will be protected cannot be guaranteed, as national treatment is generally does not apply to *sui generis* rights.

In keeping with what this book asserts in the preceding section, namely that the EU database right is a form of modified copyright, I add that a database style right for AI-generated works would also be a modified form of copyright and, as such, it would be subject to the principle of national treatment under the TRIPs agreement. Two reasons support this proposal: First, for protecting intellectual property, the TRIPs agreement covers copyright and related rights and thus suggests that the scope of protection is not limited to the works of authors, but also to investment made by phonogram producers or broadcasting organisations, which correspond with investment in AI-generated works. Second, the operation of a *sui-generis* database style right for AI-generated works would be comparable to copyright in the sense that it gives ownership to the person who has invested time, skill and money into the works. The database style right would basically extend the author's right to protect the economic interests of the contributors.[58] Including a *sui generis* database style right for AI-generated works as in the TRIPS agreement would help to set an international standard for protecting AI-generated works.

---

[57] Gaster 1995, p. 5.

[58] Ricketson 1991, p. 37.

6.3.3 *The Second Edge of the Sword: Database Protection* vis-à-vis *the Creation of AI-generated Works*

The training of generative AI software to produce AI-generated works usually relies on a large number of datasets to increase the accuracy and efficiency of the AI system's ability to create the desired output. For example, the creation of *La Comte de Belamy,* an AI-generated painting that sold for almost half a million US dollars, used 15,000 portrait paintings from the 14th to 19th centuries as training data for the algorithm.[59] Another example would be *AIVA*, a generative AI system that produces musical arrangement. AIVA is trained by over 30,000 classical music compositions.[60] A final example involves *ChatGPT,* an internet-based program known for its ability to generate human-like responses and one of the most notorious generative AI systems for producing text. The success of *ChatGPT* has largely been attributed to how well the system has been trained—a process that required OpenAI, the company which produces *ChatGPT,* to compile and use a dataset of millions of documents.[61]

Running through a large volume of data to generate new information is known as text and data mining.[62] In general, it consists of three steps, namely, 1) accessing content; 2) extracting and/or copying content; and 3) mining text and/or data and knowledge discovery.[63] The extracting and/or copying content is arguably contrary to copyright and EU's database right. Eleonora Rosati suggests that extracting and/or copying content may infringe a number of intellectual property rights. First, if the materials are sourced from a database, copyright and the *sui generis* database right may apply.[64] Second, if the extracted and/or copied materials are not included in a database, copyright and/or related rights may subsist in them.[65]

In Indonesia, which does not recognise database rights, databases are accorded copyright protection as literary works for their selection or arrangement. As such, extracting and/or copying materials from a database in Indonesia would only face copyright restrictions. In Indonesia, extracting and copying the content of database would not be considered a copyright infringement as long as it was done to advance

---

[59] Nugent 2018.

[60] European Commission—The Community Research and Development Information Service (CORDIS) 2020.

[61] On 27 December 2023, as this book was in the final stages of preparation for submission, OpenAI was sued by the New York Times in the United States for copyright violations. Specifically, the lawsuit alleges that OpenAI, along with its parent company Microsoft, had violated the plaintiff-newspaper's copyright by using its archive of previously published articles to train *ChatGPT* chat-bots. It was alleged that OpenAI had accessed, extracted, and mined the news published by The New York Times as training data and this was reflected in the chatbot's ability to answer users' questions. While this lawsuit is still on-going at the time of submission and there has been no legal judgment providing clarity, it does open up the potential for a new issue concerning copyright protection in the AI-generated works.

[62] Rosati 2018, pp. 200–202.

[63] Ibid. p. 204.

[64] Rosati 2018, p. 207.

[65] Ibid.

education, support national security, or present free-of-charge performances that did not prejudice the reasonable interests of the author.[66] In other situations, extracting and copying materials would be restricted by copyright and, possibly, other related rights. In these cases, data scientists who wanted to extract or copy materials would need to seek permission from the copyright or neighbouring rights holder. Such permission often obligates these actions to provide economic benefit to the rights holders. Paying a licensing fee to extract and/or copy materials would not be a problem when a small quantity of materials was required. Unfortunately, as text and data mining demand a vast amount of training data to be used, it would be impractical, if not impossible, to require data scientists to pay a license fee for all they use. A temporary solution would be to use copyright-free materials (i.e., works that do not qualify as copyright subject matter or where protection has expired). For example, data trainers in *La Comte de Belamy* sourced training materials from paintings whose copyright protection had already expired. Unfortunately, this approach does not provide a long-term or stable way of dealing with the clash of copyright with text and data mining not least because, if the latter were limited to materials with lapsed copyright, that would restrict the capability of generative AI to keep up with the current practices and trends.[67]

At present, data trainers are caught in the apparent deadlock between text and data mining and copyright. While data trainers need to be able to access, extract and copy materials to train the algorithms, they are faced with two problems: the first involves being able to extract and copy materials, while needing to pay an unreasonable amount of money to do so; and the second is resourcing their materials from the public domain, but risking the possibility that their training data will be outdated and thus prejudice the performance of their algorithms.

6.4 Fair Use

For advancing machine learning and artificial intelligence, steps need to be taken to untangle the conflict as to how a text relates to data mining and copyright. Some countries have devised strategies to relax copyright restrictions on text and data mining. For example, in the United States, text and data mining is often justified by fair use,[68] that is, the doctrine that allows certain uses of copyrighted materials without having to seek permissions from the copyright holder. To determine whether a particular use is a fair use, the United States Supreme Court has set the following standards:[69]

1) the purpose and the character of the use, including whether such use is of a commercial nature or is for non-profit educational purposes;

[66] Article 44, 2014 Copyright Act, above n. 15.
[67] Fiil-Flynn et al. 2022.
[68] Carroll 2019, pp. 911–912.
[69] *Campbell v Acuff Rose Music, Inc. 510 U.S., 569, 594 (1994)* in Carroll 2019.

2) the nature of copyrighted work;
3) the amount and substantiality of the portion used in relation to the copyrighted work as a whole; and
4) the effect of the use upon the potential market for or value of the copyrighted work.

These four standards were considered in *Authors Guild, Inc. v. Google, Inc.* (*Google Books*), a landmark case for fair use in the United States, in which the plaintiff complained that Google had infringed their copyright by scanning millions of books without permissions nor paying license fees.[70] The scanned books were stored on Google's server, indexed and partly displayed in Google's search engine.[71] The court held that the digitisation that assisted with the search engine result was transformative because it does not display a copy of the works. Instead, the search engine displayed only information about the works.[72] Additionally, even though Google Books copied entire books, it only shows snippets of these books in the search engine results.[73] As such, the text and data mining activities did not infringe copyright. With regard to the effect upon the potential market, the Court found that the snippets displayed as search engine results could not be seen as a substitute for the authors' books in the market. Instead, the judge decided that Google Books had actually promoted the sales and may have increased the profit of the copyright holders.[74]

Whereas Indonesian copyright law does not recognise fair use *per se*, several provisions in the Copyright law are similar to the United States fair use doctrine, that is where copying is carried out: 1) to support education, 2) to safeguard national security; 3) as a non-commercial performance; 4) to facilitate people with disabilities; or 5) altering architectural works, owing to technical concerns will not infringe as long as the acts do not jeopardise the author's reasonable interests.[75] The standard of fair use in Indonesia relies on the author's reasonable interests, which are further explained as the authors' interests to enjoy economic benefit of their works.[76] The standard is vague and subjective because it depends on the authors' view about whether they have been able to enjoy economic benefit.

In Indonesia, while fair use offers a reasonable alternative to justify the use of text and data mining, several considerations need to be made: First, a clearer test of fair use should be established because the current fair use standard in Indonesia is ambiguous. This can be seen in *PT Inter Sports Marketing v. PT Arjuna Cahaya Lestari d/a Hotel Yogyakarta* where the plaintiff paid the Federation of International Football (FIFA) for a license to air the 2014 World Cup Brazil. The defendant re-broadcast the World Cup matches without any approval or license from the plaintiff. In their defence,

---

[70] Efroni and Gebert 2011.

[71] Ibid.

[72] Woodland 2014.

[73] Ibid.

[74] Ibid.

[75] Article 44(1), 2014 Copyright Act, above n. 15.

[76] Elucidation of Article 44(1)(a), Ibid.

the defendant argued that re-broadcasting can be considered as fair use, and thus, does not infringe copyright. Budi Agus Riswandi, an expert witness for this case mentioned that reasonable interests of the author in fair use meant that using works should not be for commercial purpose.[77] While this re-broadcasting was unlawful, narrowing the standard of reasonable interests of the authors to include prohibiting any commercial use of the work is misleading. The test of fair use in the United States not only considers whether using a work is commercial, it also considers two additional factors: namely, whether the use adds new expression or meaning to the original work, and the extent to which the use substitutes for the original work in the market. Within the Google Book case, though the indexing of books could be considered commercial in nature because more users were likely to use Google as a search engine when they look for books, this does not substitute for the original work in the market. As such, it could be justified by the fair use doctrine.

Second, the fair use test may not entirely suit Indonesia because the decision about whether a use is fair depends on court decisions.[78] Two reasons clarify why court decisions in Indonesia are not a preferred option. First, as a civil law country, Indonesia does not formally accept the binding force of precedent.[79] Nevertheless, common law countries generally acknowledges that courts are bound by previous court decisions, either at the same or at a higher level.[80] Without precedent, Indonesian judges may produce different rulings for similar cases which would diminish the sense of legal certainty. Second, taking a dispute to court, especially in Indonesia, is timely and costly. A commercial court dispute of the first instance often takes up to six months.[81] Should the parties file an appeal; it may take up to two years before they receive a final and binding decision.[82]

6.5 Regulatory Exceptions Justifying Text and Data Mining

The EU Directive on Copyright in the Digital Single Market sets out several exceptions which allow for text and data mining. First, Article 3 of the Digital Single Market Directive provides that using text and data mining is not a copyright infringement if done by research organisations and cultural heritage institutions for scientific and

---

[77] *Decision of the Semarang District Court No. 2/PDT.SUS.HKI/2018/PN.Smg.*

[78] Vujicic 2022, p. 93.

[79] Butt 2022.

[80] Lindsey T, Indonesian Trial Process and Legal System, (Pt Asian Law Centre—The University of Melbourne). https://law.unimelb.edu.au/__data/assets/pdf_file/0010/1546309/Indonesians_Trial_Process_and_Legal_System_Background_Notes1.pdf. Accessed 08 January 2025.

[81] Schinder Law Firm, Settlement Agreements in Commercial Disputes during Court Proceedings in Indonesia, (Blog Post). https://schinderlawfirm.com/blog/settlement-agreements-in-commercial-disputes-during-court-proceedings-in-indonesia/.

[82] Ibid.

research purposes.[83] This is a limited exception insofar as it only applies to research organisations and cultural heritage institutions. This means that, though text and data mining was done for scientific research, it would not be exempt from copyright restriction if it was carried out by commercial companies. The exception has been criticised for failing to reflect the current research practice. Research benefiting public interests can be performed by anyone: policy makers, journalists, and commercial private actors.[84] Unfortunately, when these actors conduct text and data mining for research purposes, the Article 3 exclusion does not apply because they are neither research organisations nor cultural heritage institutions.

Article 3 of the Digital Single Market Directive, which limits users being excluded from text and data mining for scientific and research purposes, is generally contrary to the policy approach advocated in Indonesia., It is specifically contrary to the Indonesian AI National Strategy that envisages many parties, including academics, government officers, private sectors employees, and communities collaborating. The quadruple-helix collaboration enables many contributions from commercial or non-commercial users and is deemed necessary to foster public welfare, especially in education, health and infrastructure sectors. Restricting text and data mining to research organisations for education would not support Indonesia's National Strategy.

Second, under Article 4 of the Digital Single Market Directive, text and data mining are lawful if the right holders of the original work has not express any reservations.[85] If the material is created publicly available online, any reservation can be articulated in the website's terms and conditions, or through machine-readable means.[86] Machine-readable is exemplified by using robot.txt metadata that prevents indexing activities of webpages.[87] Article 4 serves as an opt-out mechanism for authors and copyright holders who do not wish their works to be used as a material for text and data mining. It offers a more general scope for them than Article 3 of the Digital Single Market Directive basically by allowing text and data mining for any purposes, by anyone, as long as no reservation has been made by the right holders.

Giving right holders an 'opt-out' mechanism prioritises private interests over public needs. Throughout history, Indonesian copyright law has taken a specific approach of balancing public and private interests, while developing AI-generated works in particular, public interests have been given more weight (as in the AI National Strategy). As such, an 'opt-out' mechanism similar to the stipulations in the EU Digital Single Market Directive would not be in favour of the public interests in Indonesia because it would limit the amount of mined data available and potentially reduce the accuracy of generative AI.

---

[83] Article 3, *Directive of the European Parliament and the Council of 17 April 2019 on Copyright and Related Rights in the Digital Single Market and Amending Directives 96/9/EC and 2001/29/EC (signed and entered into force 17 April 2019)* (EC Directive on Copyright in Digital Single Market).

[84] Ducato and Strowel 2021, p. 12.

[85] Article 4, EC Directive on Copyright in Digital Single Market, above n. 83.

[86] Ducato and Strowel 2021.

[87] Hugenholtz 2019.

6.6 Lessons Learned for Indonesia

Examples from the United States and the EU show that multiple legal mechanisms can be used to support text and data mining. Justifying text and data mining by the fair use doctrine means that any activities related to text and data mining will be allowed as long as they fall within the fair use tests. Another possibility is to exclude all text and data mining, unless it is conducted for research purposes by research organisations or cultural heritage institutions, or when right holders make no reservation is offered about text and data mining.

To date, Indonesia does not have a legal framework that allows for text and data mining. That Indonesia's AI Strategy Plan embraces the use of AI-generated works suggests that this needs to be remedied pressingly. As text and data mining are inseparable to the way AI-generated works are created, the law should be modified to allow their use to fulfil Indonesia's AI Strategy Plan.

Given that the main purpose of promoting artificial intelligence in Indonesia is to foster public needs, a less-restrictive rule for text and data mining should be adopted: one that allows use for any purpose, either commercial or non-commercial, as long as data trainers can lawfully access texts and data. This would not jeopardise the economic interests of the original owner of the work because the results of text and data mining cannot replace the original work. More relaxed measures for text and data mining are arguably more suitable for Indonesia to reduce the chance of costly and time-consuming litigation; they also support Indonesia's AI Strategy Plan to prioritise public interests.

6.7 Conclusion

While the 2008 Traditional Knowledge and Traditional Cultural Expressions Bill and the EU database right may offer important lessons for how we might craft a law to protect AI-generated works, there are a number of factors that limit their relevance. One key reason why the approach used to protect traditional cultural expressions is not a suitable model for AI-generated works is because the former typically belong to a particular community that will become the custodian of protected expressions. This is difficult to apply to AI-generated works not least because, in creating AI-generated works, stakeholders often come from different organisations. This would make it difficult to nominate a custodian for AI-generated works. Another problem is that the scope of *sui generis* rights for traditional cultural expressions are limited to national jurisdictions. In contrast, AI-generated works operate beyond geographical borders and, as a result, would benefit from uniform international protection—rather than bespoke protections that are tailored to individual creator-communities' social norms and values.

With regards to database right, the EU database right was specifically created to protect the investment necessary to create databases and to provide incentive to the industry. Two main points support this incentive: The first is that database rights are provided to parties who can demonstrate substantial investment in obtaining, verifying or presenting the contents.[88] Second, the database right only applies to databases originating from member states and from countries with reciprocal agreements with the EU that protect databases originating from its states.[89] Regarding the suggestion that the EU database right might act as a model to protect AI-generated works, this chapter finds that a database-style right presents a more feasible option to protect AI-generated works than the *sui generis* right does for traditional cultural expressions. This is because the database right has similar objectives to those needed for AI-generated works, namely to protect investment in its technology. Considering the complexity and combination of contributors' role in producing AI-generated works, this book proposes that a database-style right should be given to contributors whose investment is necessary to enable the outcomes of AI-generated works. Protecting their investment would encourage contributors to use and promote generative AI.

Despite their similarity, the EU database right cannot be directly used to protect AI-generated works because it does not apply internationally. As a tailored right, it falls outside the TRIPS agreement's so that the principle of national treatment cannot be used to demand particular jurisdictions to protect foreign nationals. However, producing, distributing and consuming AI-generated works often, if not always, transcends national boundaries thus requiring an international framework to set a standard for protecting AI-generated works. This also requires a more uniformed approach to justify text and data mining internationally. The existing justification provided by the United States and the EU are not relevant in Indonesia because they either depend on the development of court-based jurisprudence or are too restrictive. To create a conducive environment that supports the development of AI-generated works, less-restrictive rules for text and data mining internationally should be established. It is hoped that uniform and more-relaxed rules for text and data mining would promote the development of artificial intelligence.

References

Ananta A et al. (2015) Demography of Indonesia's Ethnicity. ISEAS Publishing, Singapore

Astini S M, Utina U T (2007) Tari Pendet sebagai Tari Balih-balihan (Kajian Koreografi) [Pendet Dance as a Secular Dance] . Harmonia: Journal Of Arts Research And Education 8(2):170–179 https://doi.org/10.15294/harmonia.v8i2.789

Bainbridge D I (2019) Copyright in databases. In: Information Technology and Intellectual Property Law, 7th edn. Bloomsbury Professional, Haywards Heath, pp. 178–209

Bensinger V (1999) Sui-generis Schutz für Datenbanken: die EG-Datenbankrichtlinie vor dem Hintergrund des nordischen Rechts [Sui-generis Protection for Databases: The EC Database Directive in the Context of Nordic Law]. C. H. Beck, Munich

---

[88] Article 7(1), Database Directive, above n. 25.

[89] Article 11, Ibid.

Beunen A C (2007) Protection for databases: The European Database Directive and its effects in the Netherlands, France and the United Kingdom. Wolf Legal Publishers, Nijmegen
Butt S (2022) Why do Indonesian judges dissent? Australian Journal of Asian Law 23(1):1–19
Carroll M W (2019) Copyright and the Progress of Science: Why Text and Data Mining Is Lawful. UC Davis Law Review 53:893–964
Chong J W (2012) "Mine, Yours or Ours?": The Indonesia-Malaysia Disputes over Shared Cultural Heritage. Journal of Social Issues in Southeast Asia 27(1):1–53 https://doi.org/10.1355/sj27-1a
Davison M J (1998) Sui Generis or Too Generous: Legislative Protection of Databases, Its Implications for Australia and Some Suggestions for Reform. University of New South Wales Law Journal 21(3):729–749
Derclaye E (2005) Database sui generis right: What is a substantial investment? A tentative definition. IIC: International Review of Intellectual Property and Competition Law 36(1):2–30
Ducato R, Strowel A M (2021) Ensuring text and data mining: remaining issues with the EU copyright exceptions and possible ways out. European Intellectual Property Review 43(5):322–337
Efroni Z, Gebert J (2011) The Google Books decision: The Authors Guild v Google Inc. European Intellectual Property Review 33(8):531–536
European Commission—The Community Research and Development Information Service (CORDIS) (2020) AI That Composes Complex Instrumental Music for Movies, Games, Advertising, and Other Types of Digital Media. Research Results No 421438. https://cordis.europa.eu/article/id/421438-ai-composers-create-music-for-video-games. Accessed 4 March 2022
Fiil-Flynn S M et al. (2022) Legal reform to enhance global text and data mining research. Science 378(6623):951–953 https://doi.org/10.1126/science.add6124
Gaster J L (1995) The EU Council of Ministers' Common Position Concerning the Legal Protection of Databases: A First Comment. UCLA School of Law, Los Angeles
Gosnell S (2003) Database protection down under: would a 'sweaty' Australia be better off with a northerly change? University of New South Wales Law Journal 26(3):639–679
Gupta I (2017) Footprints of Feist in European Database Directive: A Legal Analysis of IP Law-making in Europe. Springer Nature, Singapore
Hartley J (2013) Authorship and the Narrative of the Self. In: Gray J, Johnson D (eds) A Companion to Media Authorship. Wiley-Blackwell, John Wiley & Sons Ltd, Chichester, pp. 21–47 https://doi.org/10.1002/9781118505526.ch2
Hugenholtz P B (2001) The new database right: early case law from Europe. International Intellectual Property Law & Policy 7(70):1–14
Hugenholtz P B (2016) Something Completely Different: Europe's Sui Generis Database Right. In: Frankel S, Gervais D (eds) The Internet and the Emerging Importance of New Forms of Intellectual Property. Kluwer Law International, The Netherlands, pp. 205–222
Hugenholtz P B (2019) Neighbouring rights are obsolete. IIC-International Review of Intellectual Property and Competition Law 50(8):1006–1011 https://doi.org/10.1007/s40319-019-00864-3
Kariodimedjo D W (2019) Illuminating the Future by Safeguarding and Protecting Intangible Cultural Heritage in Indonesia. Doctor of Philosophy Thesis, Charles Darwin University, Australia
Lehr D, Ohm P (2017) Playing with the Data: What Legal Scholars Should Learn About Machine Learning. UC Davis Law Review 51:653–717
Maidanyk L (2021) Artificial intelligence and sui generis right: A perspective for copyright in Ukraine? Access to Justice in Eastern Europe 4(3):144–154 https://doi.org/10.33327/AJEE-18-4.3-n000076
Morrison M J (1978) The Bedaya-Serimpi Dances of Java. Dance Chronicle 2(3):188–212
Nugent C (2018) The Painter Behind These Artworks is an AI Program. Do They Still Count as Art? Time. https://time.com/5357221/obvious-artificial-intelligence-art/. Accessed 4 February 2020
Republik Indonesia (1999) Kabinet Reformasi Pembangunan: Memori Masa Bhakti [Development Reform Cabinet: Memories of Service]. Departemen Penerangan Republik Indonesia, Jakarta

Ricketson S (1991) The 1992 Horace S. Manges Lecture—People or Machines: The Berne Convention and the Changing Concept of Authorship. Columbia-VLA Journal of Law & The Arts 16(1):1

Rosati E (2018) The exception for text and data mining (TDM) in the proposed Directive on Copyright in the Digital Single Market. PE 604.942. European Parliament

Sardjono A (2004) HaKI dan Masyarakat Lokal Indonesia [Intellectual Property Rights and Indonesian Local Communities]. Indonesian Journal of International Law 2(1):147–184 https://doi.org/10.17304/ijil.vol2.1.8

Vollmer T (2018) Database Directive Study: Options for Neutralising the Sui Generis Right. Communia. https://communia-association.org/2018/05/10/database-directive-study-options-neutralising-sui-generis-right/. Accessed 21 October 2022

Vujicic N (2022). The EU copyright exceptions for text and data mining: (Un)suitable model solution for the development of artificial intelligence? Australian Intellectual Property Journal 33(2):92–106

Westkamp G (2003) TRIPS principles reciprocity and the creation of Sui-Generis-type intellectual property rights for new forms of technology. The Journal of World Intellectual Property 6(6):827–859 https://doi.org/10.1111/j.1747-1796.2003.tb00245.x

Wong T, Fernandini C (2010) Traditional cultural expressions: Preservation and innovation. In: Wong T, Dutfield G (eds) Intellectual Property and Human Development: Current Trends and Future Scenarios. Cambridge University Press, New York, pp. 175–217 https://doi.org/10.1017/CBO9780511761027.008

Woodland J (2014) Digitisation after Google Books—is fair use fair dealing? Entertainment Law Review 25(4):129

Yu R (2017) The machine author: what level of copyright protection is appropriate for fully independent computer-generated works? University of Pennsylvania Law Review 165(5):1245–1270

Chapter 7
Neighbouring Rights Protection for AI-generated Works

Contents

Abstract In searching for the most suitable model of protection for AI-generated works, this chapter argues that neighbouring rights for sound recordings and broadcasts would be the most suitable for several reasons. First, neighbouring rights focus on protecting the contributors' technological investment rather than authorship, offering more flexibility than copyright for AI-generated works. Second, neighbouring rights offer a shorter term of protection compared to copyright, allowing for a more effective balance between private and public interests. Third, neighbouring rights are universally accepted, making them more suitable for the global nature of AI-generated works compared to *sui generis* rights. This chapter proposes establishing a new type of neighbouring rights with certain specifications: 1) generative AI users as the right holders, 2) right holders are entitled solely to economic benefit from the use of AI-generated works, and 3) there should be a short term of protection for AI-generated works.

Keywords Neighbouring rights · Phonogram producers' rights · Broadcasters' rights · Private rights · Public interests · Programmers · Data trainers · Generative AI users

L. Andrini, *Protecting Artificial Intelligence-generated Works in Indonesia*, Information Technology and Law Series 41, https://doi.org/10.1007/978-94-6265-703-8_7

7.1 Introduction

In previous chapters, this book finds that AI-generated works are incompatible with Indonesian copyright law because they fail to meet the authorship and creativity requirements. I also argued that despite similarities neither domestic law protecting traditional cultural expressions nor the European Union (EU) databases rights protection provide effective templates which can be used to develop specific protection for AI-generated works. I noted that AI-generated works, like both traditional cultural expressions and databases, are often produced through collaborations involving numerous and varied stakeholders. While the *sui generis* model addressing traditional cultural expressions was specifically designed to address Indonesian legal requirements, this research finds that such a model failed as a template for considering the interests of multiple stakeholders involved in AI-generated works. The primary reason for this was because of the way that authorship was configured. Similar problems also arose with the EU database right.

This chapter shifts its focus to explore the potential of using neighbouring rights to protect AI-generated works. Specifically it assesses the possibility of using the neighbouring rights related to sound recordings and broadcasts as a template upon which to build a similar style of right for the protection of AI-generated works.[1] In doing so, I presume two conditions: the first is that creating AI-generated works requires an investment from multiple contributors and that these contributors require specific protection for their investments; the second is that the protection of AI-generated works needs to recognise the public and private interests that are jointly associated within them.

The regulation of AI-generated works invokes both public and private interests. Creating AI-generated works often involves private actors, programmers, data trainers and users. However, according to Indonesia's Strategy Plan for AI, AI-generated works also fulfil public needs pertaining to education, health, and infrastructure. These different interests are also reflected in the protection provided by neighbouring rights, as shown in Chap. 3, and embody both labour theory and economic incentive theory. As we saw, labour theory supports the private interests concerned with neighbouring rights and suggests that economic rights are given as a reward for one's labour.[2] In this context, the 'labour' comes in the form of performing a pre-existing work, investing in recording and broadcasting devices, and organising recording and broadcasting businesses. Labour theory tells us that compensation in the form of economic rights is given to offset any cost that has been borne by the performers, phonogram producers, and broadcasters while creating the works.[3] In turn, economic incentive theory prioritises public interests by saying that the main

[1] I do not consider performers' rights because they challenged copyright differently than AI-generated works. Performers' rights were created because performances do not meet the copyright requirement of fixation. Meanwhile, AI-generated works do not meet the copyright requirement of authorship and creativity, see, for example, Cohen Jehoram 1990; Sherman and Bently 1996.

[2] Hughes 1988, p. 288.

[3] Ibid.

purpose of giving monopoly rights to media entrepreneurs is to benefit the public. According to this theory, economic rights given to performers, phonogram producers, and broadcasters motivates them to produce more creations.[4] Creating and making these materials available to the public help to foster the diffusion of knowledge and information.[5]

This chapter is comprised of two sections. In the first, I discuss important aspects of the neighbouring rights in sound recordings and broadcasts by considering how technological innovations and changing socio-economic practices have influenced the policy development of neighbouring rights both internationally and in Indonesia. This allows me to describe the underlying reasons for, the nature of the rights and obligations in, and the bounds of neighbouring rights in sound recordings and broadcasts. This discussion is essential for two reasons: first, to decide whether these neighbouring rights would be a suitable model to protect AI-generated works, and second, to outline the points that will be made in the following section about how these rights might inform a similar mechanism for AI-generated works These are issues that I then directly explore in the second section of the chapter. This portion of the chapter assesses how neighbouring rights in sound recordings and broadcasts can be used as a model for developing a new type of neighbouring rights specifically crafted for AI-generated works, as well as the parameters of such a model.

7.2 Key Features of Neighbouring Rights for Sound Recordings and Broadcasts

Neighbouring rights are regulated internationally under the Rome Convention for the Protection of Performers, Producers of Phonograms, and Broadcasting Organizations of 1961 (the Rome Convention).[6] While the Convention does not use the term 'neighbouring rights', it has been widely used to address the rights to protect phonogram producers and broadcasters in many national jurisdictions, including Indonesia.

In this section, I discuss two types of the neighbouring rights, namely phonogram producers' rights and broadcasting rights. These rights protect the economic interests of phonogram producers and broadcasters rather than their moral rights because their contribution is limited to technical and financial matters.[7] In each case, I describe how the policy development surrounding those rights, including how technological advances have shaped neighbouring rights. I also consider how Indonesian law regulates these rights and how they operate in practice. Lastly, to evaluate whether these neighbouring rights could be used to construct a new type of neighbouring rights

[4] Geller et al. 1993, pp. 164–166.

[5] Senftleben and Buijtelaar 2020.

[6] *Rome Convention for the Protection of Performers, Producers of Phonograms, and Broadcasting Organizations of 1961* (the Rome Convention).

[7] Senftleben and Buijtelaar 2020.

for AI-generated works, this section compares the subject matter protected by these neighbouring rights with AI-generated works.

7.2.1 *Phonogram Producers' Rights*

In this section, I focus on the rationale behind phonogram producers' rights by investigating the reasons why special rights were needed to protect phonogram producers' rights, namely that they did not meet the copyright requirements of authorship and creativity. I then move to look at AI-generated works that similarly challenge conventional copyright to possibly construct a new type of neighbouring rights based on phonogram producers' rights to protect these works.

The invention of new sound-recording technology in the late 19th century[8] prompted discussions on the protection of phonograms during two conferences held in 1908 and 1928 that sought to revise the Berne Convention. During the conferences, the delegates explored whether using recording technologies to reproduce musical works would amount to copyright infringement, and whether phonograms could be protected as literary or artistic works under the Berne Convention.[9] While it was accepted that some sort of protection was needed, as the parties were unwilling to modify the Berne Convention to add phonograms to the works protected by copyright, it was decided that a new form of protection other than that provided by Berne was needed.

While the law had been unable to find a suitable way to protect sound recordings, inventions continued to threaten the economic interests of phonogram producers. During the 1950s and 1960s, the widespread use of home-taping devices compromised the interests of the recording companies.[10] The reason for this was that tape-recorders allowed users to record and play back audio recordings on their own without having to compensate recording companies. The widespread use of the tape recorder enabled consumers to become producers and, as a result, jeopardised producers' economic interests. In response, the Rome Convention was established in 1961 to protect phonogram producers against unfair competition by establishing an international minimum standard to protect phonogram producers.

The neighbouring rights granted to phonogram producers are based on a different rationale from the one used to justify the grant of copyright to authors. The main justification for neighbouring right is the technological investment argument, which states that producers need to be protected because they have invested heavily to establish and operate a recording business.[11] As Bernt Hugenholtz notes, the recording

[8] Davies 2012, p. 210.

[9] The first debate was brought forward at the Berne Convention Diplomatic Conference in 1886, which concluded that the recording technology did not infringe copyright. Meanwhile, the second discussion took place at the Berlin Conference in 1908, which did not result in any conclusions.

[10] Stewart and Sandison 1989.

[11] Hugenholtz 2019.

industry in the mid-20th century required investment in 'recording studios, technicians, mastering, and record manufacturing and distribution.'[12] Furthermore, as the producers' role is limited to performing technical skills in the phonogram recording, they cannot be considered as authors within the scope of conventional copyright.[13]

In Indonesia, the law related to neighbouring rights for phonogram producers, which was first introduced in 1997, is now found in the 2014 Copyright Act. This law grants phonogram producers the right to produce their works and to authorise and/or prohibit others from coping, distributing, renting and making phonograms available to the public.[14] The Act also provides producers with the right to receive equitable remuneration whenever their phonograms are used in broadcast and/or communication to the public.[15]

Neighbouring rights, particularly as they apply to phonogram producers, received significant attention when the 2014 Copyright Act was drafted. This occurred because during the early 2000s many karaoke venues in Indonesia allegedly infringed copyright and neighbouring rights by 1) using pirated copies of CDs in their businesses; 2) failing to obtain licenses/authorisations from phonogram producers; and 3) not paying royalties to producers.[16] Because recording companies in Indonesia were not compensated when their works were used, they asked for better protection of their rights during the drafting of the 2014 Copyright Act. In response, the Indonesian government created the Collective Management Organization, whose main duty is to collect and distribute royalties on behalf of copyright and neighbouring rights owners.[17]

The roles of the phonogram producers and users of AI-generated works are similar in that both perform technical and managerial roles that do not meet authorship and creativity requirement. Additionally, while they are involved in the production process and contribute to the fixation of the works, they do not necessarily produce the work. Given these similarities, neighbouring rights given to the phonogram producers could be used as a model to construct a new type of neighbouring rights for the contributors to AI-generated works.

---

[12] Ibid.

[13] Stewart and Sandison 1989.

[14] Article 24, *Law number 28 of 2014 on Copyright 2014 (Indonesia)* (2014 Copyright Act).

[15] Ibid.

[16] One of the renowned cases involved one of the biggest karaoke chains in Indonesia, Inul Vizta.

[17] *Indonesia, Parliamentary Debates at the House of Representatives on the 2014 Copyright Bill* (Parliamentary Debates). Before the 2014 Copyright Act, there were two organisations that organised the collection and distribution of royalties. Yayasan Karya Cipta Indonesia (YKCI) collected and distributed royalties for copyright owners, while Wahana Music Indonesia (WAMI) collected and distributed royalties for neighbouring rights holders. After the enactment of the 2014 Copyright Act, these organisations had to fulfil several requirements to become a Collective Management Organisation, namely: 1) obtaining an operational license from the Minister of Justice and Human Rights; 2) taking on the form of a non-profit legal entity, and 3) being authorised by at least 200 copyright/neighbouring rights owners to represent their interests, see Article 88, 2014 Copyright Act, above n. 14.

For phonogram producers' rights to function as a model for AI-generated works, some modifications would be needed. First, the protection of AI-generated works would need to consider when and how right owners were appointed, not least because producing AI-generated works involves different contributions from multiple parties. Second, as a law protecting AI-generated works needs to balance both public and private interests, the duration of protection should be shorter than the term of protection for phonograms.

Despite the similarities between phonograms and AI-generated works, the rights of the phonogram producers cannot be used to straightforwardly protect AI-generated works. One reason for this is that while a phonogram is almost always derived from an existing work (e.g., a musical composition), AI-generated works are not derivative works. In addition, while a large amount of training data is required to train the generative AI software so that the software would be able to produce works, the works themselves are not derived from the training data. The data is only used to train the algorithm so that it is able to detect and produce a desired pattern. Another difference relates to the authorship requirement which necessitates that the author's personality is reflected in the works that they create.[18] As inexplicable as it may sound, this requires that a work results directly from an author's mind. Such a requirement cannot be satisfied by AI-generated works because their main component is generally produced by generative AI software. Software users may influence the production process, but its role is usually restricted to mechanical procedures.

7.2.2 Broadcasters' Rights

Another type of neighbouring right that could be a model to protect AI-generated works is the broadcasters' rights. AI-generated works and broadcasts are alike in the sense of not meeting the copyright requirements of authorship and creativity, and that they both need protection for labour and investment made by their human contributors. Given these similarities, broadcasters' rights serve as a potential model to construct a new type of neighbouring right for AI-generated works.

Changes in recording technologies at the beginning of the 20th century not only raised concerns about protecting the rights of performers and phonogram producers, they also raised concerns about their impact on the broadcasting industry. These concerns came to a head during the 1950s and 1960s because of unauthorised re-broadcasting that was aired by other organisations without the originator's consent,[19] (e.g., broadcasts by pirate radio stations, cable networks, and the showing of sporting events in pubs, restaurants and hotels.[20]

Unauthorised broadcasting challenged the business interests of licensed broadcasters both economically and operationally. Firstly, it undermined their ability to

---

[18] Jened 2014, pp. 84–85.

[19] Stewart and Sandison 1989, p. 213.

[20] Ibid.

recoup a return for what they have 'sacrificed' or invested in establishing and running their businesses. Secondly, re-broadcasting undermined broadcasters' control of their audiences, which also has economic ramifications given their work relies heavily on license and authorisation to generate income. That is, government licences allow broadcasters to operate in disseminating information to the public[21] and their works/performances need to be authorised by the copyright owners.[22]

When it comes to fulfilling copyright requirements, broadcasters faced similar challenges to phonogram producers, because the act of broadcasting does not meet the authorship or creativity requirements under copyright law. Additionally, while broadcasters play a role in disseminating creative works, they do not create them.[23] These problems were compounded by broadcasters often airing creations that cannot be considered as 'works' in copyright law (e.g., sports programs), when their authorship and creativity need to be considered as works.[24]

Despite not being able to meet the copyright requirements, broadcasts still merit protection for several reasons. First, protection would guarantee their economic rights for what they have invested in their business. Second, the protection of broadcast would ensure that information is available to the public.[25] *In Public Ownership in Private Spectacles*, for example, Brad Sherman shows that the protection of broadcast in the United Kingdom not only safeguards the technological investment of the broadcasters, it also resolved the deadlock that prevented the dissemination of information to the public.[26] Sherman's argument is based on the deadlock that happened between the promoters of sporting events and the British Broadcasting Corporation (BBC) in the 1950s. Promoters did not allow the BBC to air sporting events because it decreased their remuneration.[27] Hence, the BBC was unable to guarantee control over the broadcast of the sporting events, nor receive more money from the public to pay the sport promoters.[28] This resulted in a ban on the broadcast of sporting events, which was only resolved after broadcasts and broadcasters were both protected.

In Indonesia, the Copyright Act[29] grants broadcasters the right to authorise or prohibit other parties from re-broadcasting, communicating, fixating, or copying the broadcast.[30] From the 2000s to the 2010s, broadcasters in Indonesia faced many issues related to the unauthorised re-broadcasting and fixation of their broadcasts.

---

[21] Ibid.

[22] Davies 2012.

[23] Ogawa 2005, p. 7.

[24] Sherman 2012, p. 231.

[25] Sherman and Wiseman 2012.

[26] Sherman 2012.

[27] Having sports events aired on television would reduce the number of spectators who would have bought tickets and attended the events. Promoters considered the payment provided by the BBC was not adequate to offset their loss in ticket sales (in ibid).

[28] Once aired, the BBC will lose control over its broadcast. Anyone with access to the broadcast and television during that time would be able to re-broadcast the sporting events without having to compensate the BBC (in ibid).

[29] Article 25, 2014 Copyright Act, above n. 14.

[30] Article 25 (2), Ibid.

Cafes, restaurants, and hotels broadcast football matches without paying royalties to the owner of the broadcasting rights.[31] To protect broadcasters, the 2014 Copyright Act incorporates regulations on the role of the Collective Management Organisation to collect and distribute royalties to copyright and neighbouring rights owners, including broadcasters. The Collective Management Organisation represents the interests of broadcasters both nationally and internationally.

One reason for granting neighbouring rights to broadcasters was to ensure the public interest in disseminating information. Similarly, AI-generated works, especially in Indonesia, also serve the public interest, such as using AI-generated works to support education, as envisaged in Indonesia's National Strategic Plan for AI. Protecting these works serves as an incentive for private parties to disseminate more information and knowledge to the public. Despite this, broadcasts and AI-generated works differ significantly because broadcasts are derivative works that are based upon pre-existing works, such as, musical arrangements, motion pictures, or sound recordings,[32] and are thus already protected by copyright. As such, broadcasters need to obtain licenses from the copyright holder to transmit them. In contrast, AI-generated works cannot be classified as derivative because they do not contain protected elements of expression from the primary work.[33] While large amounts of data are needed to train the machine-learning algorithms, the resulting AI-generated works are not derived from that data.

7.3 A New Type of Neighbouring Rights for AI-generated Works?

AI-generated works are similar to works protected under neighbouring rights in that they are unable to meet copyright requirements, but nonetheless still require protection. To the extent that AI-generated works are created by generative AI software, it is also unlikely that AI-generated works will meet copyright's authorship requirements. Specifically, it is unlikely that AI-generated works would satisfy the requirement that an author be a legal person and that the authors personality is reflected in the work. Further, AI-generated works cannot fulfil the creativity requirement given that their production is more mechanical than creative.[34]

Despite the similarities, AI-generated works do not fall withing the scope of neighbouring rights protection. While the neighbouring rights for the producers of phonograms and broadcasters protect derivative works, AI-generated works are not derived from other works. Therefore, because of such differences, the existing neighbouring

[31] Parliamentary Debates, above n. 17.

[32] Wu 1997, pp. 139–140.

[33] Samuelson 1986, pp. 1211–1215.

[34] There have been debates around this notion, arguing that computer software can be creative too. See Bridy 2012.

rights cannot be used in a straightforward manner so as to provide protection for AI-generated works. At best, they serve as a model or template of protection that might be adopted to accommodate AI-generated works. A new type of neighbouring right that is distinct from the current rights for phonogram producers and broadcast organisations is needed. In thinking about the nature of the law to protect AI-generated works, three important features need to be considered; namely, who the right holders are, the scope of the economic rights, and the duration of protection.

7.3.1 *Neighbouring Right Holders*

As discussed in Chap. 2, creating AI-generated works generally involves multiple parties including programmers, data trainers and software users. However, not all these parties should be considered as owners of AI-generated works. There are two reasons for this. First, since the parties often come from different corporations or organisations, it would be impractical to nominate all the parties as owners of AI-generated works: especially when it comes to distributing economic rights and drawing liability among the parties. Second, some of these parties already received copyright protection for their labour, such as programmers or software companies owning copyright for the generative AI that they made. Data trainers usually also own copyright over databases they collected and arranged. Consequently, if they were given rights over AI-generated works it would probably over-reward them.[35] Therefore, this section considers who, among the programmers, data trainers and users, should be the most suitable party to own AI-generated works.

Given the skill, time and effort that each of these parties invests in creating AI-generated works, there are good arguments why their economic rights should be acknowledged. First, programmers and data trainers contribute to creating the generative AI software that is capable of producing the works. In most cases, programmers determine the function of the software and create the algorithm to perform that function,[36] while data trainers collect and refine the extensive training data used to train the algorithm so it can create the desired results.[37] Programmers and data trainers also contribute extensively to creating the generative AI software. Software users take part in the creation of the works insofar as they invest financially in purchasing the software. They also decide when and how frequently the software should create AI-generated works and finalise the works to ensure that they are market-ready, by selecting, editing, and fixing them in a tangible medium.

The role of programmers, data trainers, and software users is not absolute: what they add varies depending on the type and purpose of the AI-generated work in question. When discussing generative AI producing scarf patterns earlier, I showed that different parties performed distinct roles. I also showed how users are widely

[35] Yu 2017, p. 1245.
[36] Lehr and Ohm 2017, p. 681.
[37] Ibid.

involved in editing, selecting, and printing the pattern. In other contexts, the different roles may be performed by a collective, such as when generative AI are trained, developed, and executed to create artworks in *Obvious* Art.

Because of these varied roles, it is often difficult to identify a coherent group of rights holders and to draw a line between the responsibilities within AI-generated works. Under Indonesian law, neighbouring rights should be attributed to the party who contributes to the final work. Such an attribution would honour anyone who has made a creative and economic contribution to the AI-generated works, such as the person who provided hardware supplies, paid the employees' salary, or supplied the raw materials.[38]

To determine whose investment in creating AI-generated works needs to be protected, we need to consider the 'labour' of each contributor, and whether incentives have already been provided for them. The programmers' role is essential in establishing the generative AI software and determining its capabilities. Programmers are almost always considered to be the authors of the software. The copyright that exists in the software functions as both as an incentive and compensation for investment. Significantly, data trainers train generative AI software, but, if they belong to the same corporation or institution as the programmers, they are automatically considered to 'own' the program. However, where data trainers come from a different entity, the programmers usually purchase the training data from these trainers. Hence, while they are not considered as owners of the work, their labour has already been compensated by the earnings they obtained from the sale of the training data.

Users take part in executing the generative AI software to produce AI-generated works. Their contribution to the AI-generated work will depend on how autonomous the software is. While some users help to create AI-generated works, others contribute little when they prompt the generative AI to create works autonomously. Even though users may invest in creating AI-generated works, both financially and non-financially, Indonesian law has no means to compensate them for their investment. To remedy this, users should be recognised as the most suitable party to own the neighbouring rights in AI-generated works.

7.3.2 Rights for the Neighbouring Rights Holder

Conventional copyright grants both moral rights and economic rights to owners. Conversely, neighbouring rights do not necessarily come with moral and economic rights, nor do they offer the same level of protection traditionally associated with copyright. The protection given to AI-generated works should only comprise economic rights, and not moral rights, because no 'real' author is associated with producing AI-generated works. Generative AI software, which produces the works,

[38] This is based on the example of a fashion design business in Indonesia that uses generative AI software to create patterns for their scarfs, as discussed in Chap. 2 of this book.

cannot be deemed as an author because it is not a legal subject within the scope of Indonesian copyright law. Further, the software users, who have taken part in selecting, editing, fixating and publishing the work, cannot establish an authorial connection with the AI-generated works because the works are not their personal expressions.

Attributing economic rights in AI-generated works can be justified by both labour and incentive theory. Regarding AI-generated works, contributors perform a series of tasks that justify their being granted economic interest over the works. Additionally, protecting AI-generated works serves as an incentive to contributors to use the generative AI software and to create more works in the future. The protection given to phonogram producers and broadcasters serves as an incentive for them to produce more works that encourages knowledge and information to be circulated. One commentator argues that incentive theory does not apply to AI-generated works because they are automatically generated by machine.[39] As a result, providing an incentive is irrelevant because machines will produce works even if no protection is provided for them.

The problem with this argument is that it does not accurately represent how AI-generated works are created. As I showed in Chap. 1, creating AI-generated works demands labour from programmers, data trainers and software users. Programmers and/or data trainers generally make a substantive investment in the research, development, and distribution of generative AI software. They project how a software should function, collect data as training materials, train the software to generate data, and repair any problem that occurs in the software. Then, users also make an important contribution by buying the software, by initiating the production process using generative AI software, and by finalising the AI-generated works so that they are publicly available. The participation of these parties thwarts the common misunderstanding that creating AI-generated works does not require a human contribution. As such, protecting AI-generated works can be justified by labour theory.

7.3.3 Duration of Protection

The duration of protection for neighbouring rights is shorter than that provided by copyright. According to the Rome Convention 1961, the minimum period of protection is 20 years after the first performance, fixation or broadcast of works.[40] In contrast, copyright works are generally protected for 70 years after the death of the author. The shorter period of protection for neighbouring rights was set to provide equitable remuneration for the technological investment made by producers of phonograms and broadcasters.[41] Twenty years is considered a long enough period of time to allow producers and broadcasters to recoup these investments.

---

[39] Schönberger 2018.

[40] Article 14, The Rome Convention, above n. 6.

[41] Hugenholtz 2019, pp. 1007–1008.

A new neighbouring right specifically tailored to protect AI-generated works would provide right holders with the opportunity to receive a return on their investment. As explained in the previous section, creating AI-generated works requires investments from multiple parties: programmers needing resources to generate codes, data trainers needing a large amount of training data; and users, despite their varying contributions, being usually required to make a one-off payment or periodical subscription to use generative AI software.[42]

This research does not propose to calculate the exact duration of protection for two reasons. First, the research is not supported by data regarding the cost of creating AI-generated work, nor is supported by data showing the profit produced by using AI-generated works. Second, the cost and benefit of creating AI-generated works may vary depending on the scale of production and the purpose of the works. Those produced experimentally needs considerably a lower cost of production than works produced on a larger scale and thus an accurate calculation that represents the realistic conditions in the field cannot be assessed.

Although an exact calculation would be difficult to determine without further analysis, I would argue that as a matter of policy, the term of protection for AI-generated works should be shorter than the broadcasters' and phonogram producers' rights. There are two reasons for this: first, the cost of producing AI-generated works is arguably lower than the cost of producing broadcasts and sound recordings. For example, a web-based generative AI software sets a price of EUR 33 [~51 AUD] per month for users to create music compositions using their software. This is much lower than the cost of running a conventional broadcast or recording studio.[43] As such, the period needed to acquire equitable remuneration should also be shorter. Second, AI-generated works in Indonesia also aim to support public welfare. A short period of protection would better serve to balance public and private interests.

7.4 Conclusion

The process of creating AI-generated works is not entirely autonomous. In fact, at the current machine learning capacity, human authors still need to make the works available to the public. In this regard, the role of the software user is similar to phonogram producers and broadcasters in that they play a part in fixing the works into a tangible medium and publishing them. Despite the contribution made by humans in creating AI-generated works, protecting them with copyright cannot be justified, mainly because the authorship and creativity requirement cannot be met. However, leaving AI-generated works to the public domain would also be undesirable as it could potentially reduce the use of generative AI software that is capable of creating

[42] Web-based generative AI software offers subscription plans ranging from a fee of AUD 20 up to AUD 100 per month.

[43] More contemporary methods of broadcasting and recording also need a small amount of investment.

AI-generated works and, at the same time, increase fake copyright claims over AI-generated works. To prevent this from happening, my proposal is to construct a new type of neighbouring right specifically tailored to protect AI-generated works.

In many ways neighbouring rights offer a more flexible mode of protection than copyright. It protects the contributors' economic interests by prioritising their ability to recoup on their investment in the creation of a work instead of preventing others from using it.[44] In relation to creating and using AI-generated works in Indonesia, neighbouring rights are able to balance public and private interests. They acknowledge the need of private parties to be compensated fairly for, and profit from, their investment in AI-generated works. At the same time, it would also encourage knowledge and information to be circulated to the public.

There are three other reasons why protecting AI-generated works by neighbouring rights would be beneficial. First, a new neighbouring right for AI-generated works would not only provide a reward to contributors, it would also make them liable for anything related to the AI-generated works. Owing to its automated nature, AI-generated works may possibly contain defamatory material or infringe existing works. Should the AI-generated works go unprotected into the public domain, nobody would take responsibility for such offences. In contrast, when contributors hold neighbouring rights over AI-generated works, they would be expected to control the content of the works before it is fixated and circulated to the public. As a result, they would be responsible for the content.

Second, neighbouring rights offer a shorter term of protection than copyright, meaning that works under their protection would be in the public domain sooner than works protected by copyright. In the Indonesian Copyright Act, performers and producers of phonograms enjoy 50 years of protection after the fixation of the works, while broadcasting organisations enjoy 20 years after their first broadcast.[45] These durations are shorter than the term for copyright (i.e., 70 years after the passing of the author).[46] The duration of protection for AI-generated works would need to be gauged to ensure that users are equitably remunerated for their contribution.

Third, neighbouring rights are a universally recognised form of protection. This would increase the possibility that the production and use of AI-generated works would not be restricted to one country. The global nature of AI-generated works means that a universally-acknowledged form of protection that transcends national borders is needed. Compared to *sui generis* rights whose application may be limited to a certain jurisdiction, neighbouring rights can be applied to multiple jurisdictions, thus providing legal certainty to those associated in some way with creating and using AI-generated works.

---

[44] Senftleben and Buijtelaar 2020.

[45] Article 63, 2014 Copyright Act, above n. 14.

[46] Article 58, ibid.

References

Bridy A (2012) Coding Creativity: Copyright and the Artificially Intelligent Author. Stanford Technology Law Review 5:1–28

Cohen Jehoram H (1990) The nature of neighboring rights of performing artists, phonogram producers and broadcasting organizations. Columbia-VLA Journal of Law & the Arts 15(1):75

Davies G (2012) The 50th anniversary of the Rome Convention for the protection of performers, producers of phonograms and broadcasting organisations: reflections on the background and importance of the Convention. Queen Mary Journal of Intellectual Property 2(3):206–224

Geller P E et al. (eds) (1993) International copyright law and practice. Matthew Bender, New York

Hugenholtz P B (2019) Neighbouring rights are obsolete. IIC—International Review of Intellectual Property and Competition Law 50(8):1006–1011 https://doi.org/10.1007/s40319-019-00864-3

Hughes J (1988) The Philosophy of Intellectual Property. Georgetown Law Journal 77(2):287

Jened R (2014) Hukum Hak Cipta [Copyright Law]. Citra Aditya Bakti, Bandung

Lehr D, Ohm P (2017) Playing with the Data: What Legal Scholars Should Learn About Machine Learning. UC Davis Law Review 51:653–717

Ogawa M (2005) Protection of broadcasters' rights. Brill, The Netherlands https://doi.org/10.1163/ej.9789004150287.i-202

Samuelson P (1986) Allocating Ownership Rights in Computer-Generated Works. University of Pittsburgh Law Review 47:1185–1228

Schönberger D (2018) Deep Copyright: Up- and Downstream Questions Related to Artificial Intelligence (AI) and Machine Learning (ML). Droit d'auteur 4.04 / Copyright 4.0 145–173

Senftleben M, Buijtelaar L (2020) Robot creativity: an incentive-based neighboring rights approach. European Intellectual Property Review 42(12):797–812

Sherman B (2012) Public ownership of private spectacles. In: Sherman B, Wiseman L (eds) Copyright and the Challenge of the New. Kluwer Law International, The Netherlands, pp. 221–249

Sherman B, Bently L (1996) Performers Rights: Options for Reform, 1st edn. Dept. Communication & Arts, Canberra

Sherman B, Wiseman L (eds) (2012) Copyright and the challenge of the new. Kluwer Law International B.V., The Netherlands

Stewart S M, Sandison H R (1989) International Copyright and Neighbouring Rights, 2nd edn. Butterworth

Wu A J (1997) From Video Games to Artificial Intelligence: Assigning Copyright Ownership to Works Generated by Increasingly Sophisticated Computer Programs. AIPLA Quarterly Journal 25(1):131–178

Yu R (2017) The machine author: what level of copyright protection is appropriate for fully independent computer-generated works? University of Pennsylvania Law Review 165(5):1245–1270

Chapter 8
Regulatory Options to Accommodate AI-generated Works

Contents

Abstract This chapter reviews the findings and discussions explored in the previous chapters to support the main argument of this book, namely that AI-generated works require protection because human contributors are involved in their production. However, copyright as it stands cannot protect them because they fail to meet both the authorship and creativity requirement. Additionally, the *sui generis* right, such as the EU database right, lacks universal applicability for protecting AI-generated works. Therefore, this book proposes a construction of a new type of neighbouring right to accommodate AI-generated works for two reasons: first, neighbouring rights protect investment rather than an authorial contribution, and second, they are universally applicable.

Keyword AI-generated works · Artificial intelligence · Neighbouring rights · Copyright · *sui generis* right · Economic rights · Moral rights

8.1 Examining Approaches within Copyright and Neighbouring Rights

This book explores several possibilities of claiming proprietary rights for AI-generated work. It begins with discussing the novel challenges brought by AI-generated works to copyright in Chap. 1. It identifies that AI-generated works do not fit into copyright's requirement of authorship and creativity. In responding to those challenges, scholarly debates and regulatory shifts are inevitable. Unfortunately, the shifting of regulation is often carried out as a temporary solution instead of a permanent answer to the challenge brought by generative AI to copyright. In the long run, this short-term strategy would confuse people involved in developing

L. Andrini, *Protecting Artificial Intelligence-generated Works in Indonesia*, Information Technology and Law Series 41, https://doi.org/10.1007/978-94-6265-703-8_8

AI-generated works, such as: artists, software developers, and users of generative AI, especially as to whether their works are protected.

In searching for consistent legal frameworks to accommodate AI-generated works, the discussion in Chap. 2 focuses on the process of creating generative AI and AI-generated works. Understanding the process is essential to clarify common misinterpretation that generative AI runs autonomously and does not involve human interests and participation. In fact, creating and operating generative AI generally involve a lot of people, where overlapped interests are often inevitable.

Chapter 3 lays out the main reasons why AI-generated works need to be protected. It emphasises that such protection is aimed to reward and compensate human contributors who train, control, and utilise the software. This argument is justified by both natural and utilitarian approaches in intellectual property law. This chapter also recommends that the proprietary owner of an AI-generated work should be its human contributor, for example: generative AI user. It argues that giving proprietary rights to a human contributor is a better option for two main reasons. First, it compensates and rewards the contributors for any efforts and/or financial investment they have performed. Second, it establishes the owner's responsibility for any materials they circulate to the public.

In assessing whether copyright would serve as the right mechanism to protect AI-generated works, Chap. 4 of this book explores economic and moral rights of copyright. It finds that only economic rights can be assigned to the human contributors of AI-generated works. Meanwhile, moral rights cannot be passed because they necessitate an inseparable connection between the authors and their works. As a result, moral rights may not be present in the AI-generated works due to the absence of a direct connection between the generative AI users and AI-generated works. Additionally, moral rights cannot be given to the generative AI because it does not have personality that can be reflected into the works.

As the creation of AI-generated works involve many stakeholders performing specified roles, Chap. 5 tries to find who, among those stakeholders, should have control over and receive benefit from the utilisation of AI-generated works. In doing so, the analysis is based on copyright's authorship, economic and moral rights. It finds that the attribution of moral rights in AI-generated works is almost impossible because to be considered an author of a work, Indonesian copyright law requires that the author's personality be reflected in the work. Failing to establish the authorial status, he/she would not be entitled to moral rights.

The creators of AI-generated works, however, may have economic rights. Economic rights are authors' exclusive rights to gain benefit from the utilisation of the work.[1] However, the economic rights often limit the number of its authors. Meanwhile, the creation of AI-generated works may involve a large number of contributors. This leads to the question of whether multiple authorship for AI-generated works is possible. The answer to this question is based on the Indonesia's bill on *sui generis* right for traditional knowledge and traditional cultural expressions as a model of protecting AI-generated works. In *sui generis* right for traditional knowledge and

[1] *Law number 28 of 2014 on Copyright 2014 (Indonesia)* (2014 Copyright Act), Article 8. F.

traditional cultural expressions, works are collectively owned and managed by a community who originates or lives in a particular place. It could not be the suitable model for protecting AI-generated works because their developers, data trainers, and users often come from different institutions. Making all of them custodian of the AI-generated works, parallel to the custodian community of traditional knowledge or traditional cultural expressions, is not efficient as it would increase the management and production cost of AI-generated works.

Another model to protect AI-generated works, as explored in Chap. 6, is the EU *sui generis* database right. This right is constructed to protect any investments needed in the creation and management of database. As such, it does not require any authorial input as a condition of protection. *Sui generis* database right makes an optimal model for the protection of AI-generated works as they do not need to meet the authorship and creativity requirement. The only problem of protecting AI-generated works with *sui generis* right is the lack of international uniformity and applicability. As a specially-tailored right, each national jurisdiction may have their own approach in establishing the *sui generis* framework to protect AI-generated works. They cannot compel other countries to comply with their own standard. Unfortunately, such circumstances will not be suitable for AI-generated works as their production, distribution, and consumption often transcends national borders.

As neither the *sui generis* right for traditional cultural expressions nor *sui generis* database protection are applicable for the protection of AI-generated works, Chap. 7 of this book explores the possibility of modelling neighbouring rights. It finds that neighbouring rights could be a suitable model for protecting AI-generated works for three reasons. First, neighbouring rights draw a line of responsibility between users and the AI-generated works. Second, neighbouring rights offer a shorter term of protection than copyright. They become an essential element to balance public and private rights, as the works will become available to the public sooner than copyrighted works. Third, neighbouring rights are universally acknowledged. They guarantee legal certainty among stakeholders involved in the production of AI-generated works. Even though neighbouring rights contain a greater possibility as a model for protecting AI-generated works, there is one underlying difference that means they cannot be applied directly to AI-generated works. Neighbouring rights protect derivative works, while AI-generated works are not derivative works. The production of AI-generative works, indeed, requires a lot of training data. However, those data are only used to train the generative AI-algorithm. As such, AI-generated works are not derived from the training data.

The discussion in this book stresses the need to construct a new type of neighbouring rights that gives the rights to generative AI users. The users are given economic rights because they put both labour and monetary investment into the production process of AI-generated works. However, they cannot be attributed with moral rights because there is no authorial connection between the users and the work. The new concept of neighbouring rights could also give a short term of protection to balance public and private interests surrounding AI-generated works.

8.2 Adapting Neighbouring Rights to Protect AI-generated Works

In January 2023, three visual artists in the United States filed a class-action lawsuit against Stability AI, Midjourney, and DeviantArt, a group of generative AI developers, in which the plaintiffs allege the defendants infringed their copyright by using their artworks as training data without their consent.[2] The infringement claim was promptly dismissed because the artists failed to demonstrate the similarity between the infringing works (which were AI-generated) and their 'original' artworks. As such, the court determined that copyright infringement could not be established.[3] Similarly, on 3 November 2022, a lawsuit was filed against GitHub, Microsoft, and OpenAI because their AI-based tool, Copilot, allegedly violated both open-source licenses and copyright law.[4] Copilot, a programming assistance tool powered by OpenAI, helps users to complete lines of source code.[5] The plaintiffs in this lawsuit allege that Copilot-assisted software development uses codes available in GitHub in a manner that goes beyond the scope of their open-source licenses. Additionally, Copilot also allegedly infringed the original coder's copyright by omitting the copyright management information of the original code.[6]

Disputes of this nature involving generative AI systems are proliferating around the world and this will continue until there is clarity about the nature of the proprietary interests in generative AI works. To date, some jurisdictions have introduced regulations on text and data mining.[7] For example, the EU sets a restrictive standard on text and data mining, while the United States relies on fair use to justify text and data mining.[8] Meanwhile, Japan has established a relaxed rule on text and data mining[9] that is based upon that jurisdiction's legal principle that copyright only afford protection to the extent of the enjoyment of the work. As such, an exploitation of works for the purpose of generative AI training does not amount to an enjoyment of the work and should, therefore, be exempted from copyright protection.[10] Taking into account Indonesia's strategic goals for developing generative AI systems and producing AI-generated works for public needs, it should consider recognising copyright or some similar right for text and data mining. Further, Indonesian government

---

[2] *Sarah Andersen, et al., v. Stability AI LTD., et al., United States District Court, Northern District of California, Case No. 23-cv-00201-WHO.*

[3] Ibid.

[4] *J. Doe 1, et al., v. GITHUB, INC., et al., United States District Court, Northern District of California, Case No. 22-cv-06823-JST.*

[5] Mello 2023.

[6] Copyright management information is, for example, copyright notices, authors' names, copyright owners' names, terms and conditions, and identifying numbers of the code.

[7] See Dermawan 2024 and Ueno 2021.

[8] Carroll 2019.

[9] Singapore allows text and data mining for all purposes, while Japan allows the exploitation of works as long as it is not aimed at enjoyment purposes.

[10] Ueno 2021, p. 150.

also needs to outline and clearly articulate such right to allow for legal certainty and clarity.

It is also important that Indonesia clarify the state's position regarding the protection that AI-generated works should receive. In exploring this question, this book began by arguing that copyright is not the best tool to protect AI-generated works because they cannot fulfil the requirements of authorship and creativity.[11] Moreover, allowing copyright in AI-generated works is also not ideal for Indonesia given that such proprietary interests prioritise private, individualised creators at the expense of the public interest in protected works. Given that Indonesian policy is currently promoting the use of generative AI and the creation of generative AI-works in certain public sectors—such as education and health—a balance prioritizing private interests over public developmental goals is not ideal.[12]

Given this, in searching for the most appropriate form of protection for AI-generated works that can accommodate Indonesia's interests, this book explored other type of proprietary rights surrounding copyright, namely *sui generis* rights and neighbouring rights. In relation to *sui generis* right, this book finds that even though the database right may be a potential model of protection, its lack of international applicability means that it is not suitable to protect AI-generated works, whose creation process often transcends national borders. Additionally, it considered whether Indonesia's *sui generis* protections for traditional cultural expressions could be an appropriate template for recognizing stakeholder interests in AI-generated works. This book rejected this possibility because while both types of work can be viewed as the products of hyper-authored collaborations, the way in which collective rights in traditional cultural expressions were managed under this *sui generis* model does not reflect the social relationships underlying the production of AI-generated works.

Given these problems, this research then turned to look at neighbouring rights as a potential model for new laws to protect AI-generated works. In my opinion, neighbouring rights are an appropriate mechanism for providing the limited but necessary protection required to encourage AI-generated works in the public interest. As such, neighbouring rights for AI-generated works should be given to those stakeholders that have contributed labour and invested resources for the production of AI-generated works. Specifically, such neighbouring rights should be given for a limited time that is of lesser duration than the typical copyright term. This would allow the AI-generated works to pass more quickly into the public domain, enabling enhanced access. The neighbouring rights in AI-generated works should be limited only to economic rights and not include moral rights, given the absence of authorial contributions. Furthermore, economic rights would be allocated to stakeholders in recognition of their labours and investment. A final reason why neighbouring rights are better suited to protect AI-generated works is because, unlike *sui generis* rights,

[11] Lucchi 2023.

[12] James Boyle even suggested that copyright should be the exception, and not the norm, due to its restrictive nature, see Boyle 2008, p. 193.

they have been universally-accepted by most countries in the world—thus, providing a basis for international harmonisation.

A neighbouring rights framework for the protection of AI-generated works would not only benefit Indonesia. As neighbouring rights are universally recognised, it would also offer mutual benefits for other countries. For example, AI-generated works produced in Indonesia could be protected by neighbouring rights both in Indonesia and in other countries. Similarly, AI-generated works produced outside Indonesia could also be protected by neighbouring rights in Indonesia. This mechanism arguably offers a better protection than a rejecting the protection of AI-generated works on the ground that they are made without human intervention. In fact, as suggested in this book, the production of AI-generated works require a lot of human contributions that needs to be recognised and rewarded.

Generative AI systems and their related works have the potential to radically change the way Indonesians create and what they consume and use. Developing this potential is a strategic policy priority for the Indonesian state as it moves towards the future. As part of this transition, it is important that the law ensures that AI-generated creations are protected in a manner that cultivates their production in the public interest. Furthermore, any attempt to cultivate this should be done in a way that broadly supports Indonesian policy goals and aspirations. There is little doubt that generative AI will continue to change and, as a result, continue to present complex challenges for the law. While aspects of the technology may change and, in doing so, demand ongoing shifts in copyright law, it is important to keep in mind that any legal changes that are made must also accommodate the broader socio-economic interests as well the expectations of individual stakeholders.

References

Boyle J (2008) The Public Domain: Enclosing the Commons of the Mind. Yale University Press, London

Carroll M W (2019) Copyright and the Progress of Science: Why Text and Data Mining Is Lawful. UC Davis Law Review 53:893–964

Dermawan A (2024) Text and data mining exceptions in the development of generative AI models: What the EU member states could learn from the Japanese "nonenjoyment" purposes? The Journal of World Intellectual Property 27(1):44–68 https://doi.org/10.1111/jwip.12285

Lucchi N (2023) ChatGPT: A Case Study on Copyright Challenges for Generative Artificial Intelligence Systems. European Journal of Risk Regulation 2023:1–23 https://doi.org/10.1017/err.2023.59

Mello D R et al. (2023) Insights from the Pending Copilot Class Action Lawsuit. Bloomberg Law

Ueno T (2021) The Flexible Copyright Exception for 'Non-Enjoyment' Purposes—Recent Amendment in Japan and Its Implication. GRUR International 70(2):145–152 https://doi.org/10.1093/grurint/ikaa184

Index

L. Andrini, *Protecting Artificial Intelligence-generated Works in Indonesia*, Information Technology and Law Series 41, https://doi.org/10.1007/978-94-6265-703-8

MIX
Papier aus verantwortungsvollen Quellen
Paper from responsible sources
FSC® C105338

If you have any concerns about our products,
you can contact us on
ProductSafety@springernature.com

In case Publisher is established outside the EU,
the EU authorized representative is:
Springer Nature Customer Service Center GmbH
Europaplatz 3, 69115 Heidelberg, Germany

Printed by Libri Plureos GmbH
in Hamburg, Germany